Heart Healthy Cookbook for Beginners

2000 days of Heart Healthy tasty & easy Recipes,Low Sodium, Low Fat, Recipes made to reduce Cholesterol & Blood Pressure, Improved with a 90-Day Meal Plan & Guides for continuing Heart Healthy lifestyle.

Marianna S.

Copyright

Disclaimer Notice:

The recipes and suggestions in this book are intended for informational and educational purposes only and are not intended to replace the advice, diagnosis, or treatment of a qualified healthcare provider. Always consult your physician or other qualified health provider with any questions you may have regarding a medical condition.

The author and publisher are not responsible for any adverse effects or consequences resulting from the use of any recipes, suggestions, or procedures described in this book. While the recipes included are designed to be heart-healthy, individual dietary needs and health conditions vary; thus, it is crucial to consult with a healthcare professional before making significant changes to your diet. The author has made every effort to ensure that the information in this book is accurate and up-to-date as of the publication date. However, medical knowledge is constantly evolving, and the author does not assume any liability for errors, omissions, or future changes in the recommendations.

Table Of Content

Welcome to your Heart healthy journey

Hello

This book is intended for both beginners and those who are well versed in the topic.

Welcome to the "Heart Healthy Cookbook for Beginners' ': I believe you bought this cookbook because you are sincere in your decision and want to have a great effect on your heart health. In order for your meal plan to work, you must focus on the fact that it should be a "90-Day Meal Plan".This book is designed to guide you on a transformative journey towards better heart health through delicious, nutritious, and easy-to-prepare meals.Proper nutrition can significantly reduce the risk of developing cardiovascular issues and prevent existing heart problems from worsening. Additionally, a healthy diet can help avoid various cardiac troubles and illnesses, except, of course, those of a romantic nature ;).

By Marianna S.

Heart health is crucial because the heart is the central organ responsible for pumping blood throughout the body, delivering oxygen and nutrients to tissues, and removing waste products. Good heart health ensures that all body systems function properly, reduces the risk of cardiovascular diseases such as heart attacks and strokes, and enhances overall quality of life. Maintaining a healthy heart through a balanced diet, regular exercise, and avoiding harmful habits like smoking can lead to a longer, more active, and fulfilling life.

Why Heart Health Matters

Cardiovascular disease is one of the most vital parts of the human body which most individuals do not pay attention to until they experience difficulties. As heart disease is known to be the number one killer worldwide, it becomes important to give proper attention to heart issues to avoid such losses. According to WHO, cardiovascular diseases are estimated to account for 17 million deaths annually. 9 million people every year. This statistic raises awareness and action which is paramount. The heart is one of the important organs in the human body that has the central role of pumping blood all over the body supplying it with oxygen and nutrients and removing at the same time waste products. Some of the diseases that affect the heart include coronary artery disease, heart attack, irregular heartbeats, and heart failure. These conditions can all have a very detrimental effect on the heart and its ability to perform properly.

It should be noted that heart health is not only an issue of the cardiovascular system, but the overall functioning of every bodily organ. Coronary artery disease is characterized by decreased life quality as physical activity can be strenuous due to angina, shortness of breath, and fatigue. The economic and social impacts are also of great concern through increased healthcare expenditure and burden placed on families and carers. Also, heart diseases have a close connection with other diseases and ailments. Diabetes, hypertension, and obesity are some of the diseases closely related to cardiovascular health and the two continuously feed each other.

There are numerous risk indicators of heart disease, which include genetic and hereditary risk indicators. These factors include undesirable diet, physical inactivity, smoking, and excessive taking of alcohol. The risk rises with other medical conditions such as diabetes and hypertension. It is therefore important to adopt measures that will help protect the heart. It has been demonstrated that regular consumption of fruits, vegetables, whole grain and lean meats can help to reduce heart diseases. Pertaining to the cardiovascular system, physical exercise like walking, running, or swimming helps build up the strength of the heart and increases blood flow. Smoking should be abandoned and alcohol intake should be moderate if it has to be at all. This can be as a result of frequent medical check ups and fo low ups as a way of screening for early signs of heart diseases.

Caring for the health of the heart has a significant impact, which is why it is crucial to follow certain guidelines. It can result in increased life span and outcomes with relatively higher expectancy. Another added value involves improvements in both physical and mental health as the heart being healthy translates to better physical performance and brain capacity. In addition, addressing, and improving heart health, we can lower the expenses and the burden on the health care system. In conclusion, stressing on the significance of heart health again drives home the point that making efforts towards prevention is a way of adding more quality years to our lives. Hence by knowing the type of risk, one can also prevent the risk factors and therefore lower the chances of heart disease and thus improve the quality of our life.

How Diet Impacts Heart Health

Diet plays a crucial role in maintaining and improving heart health. The choices we make every day regarding the food we consume can either protect or harm our cardiovascular system.Research consistently shows that diet is one of the most significant factors influencing heart health. Consuming a balanced diet rich in nutrients can help reduce the risk of heart disease, lower cholesterol levels, and maintain healthy blood pressure.

Cholosterol Levels Before and after Diffrent diets

Y Cholosterol Level by X Diet for ■ Before and ■ After

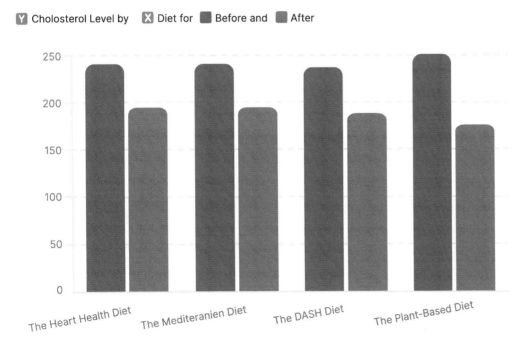

Improvement Of Blood Pressure Over Time By Diet

Y Blood Pressure (mmHg) X Week for ■ Heart Health Diet, ■ Mediteranean Diet,
■ DASH Diet, and ■ Plant -Based Diet

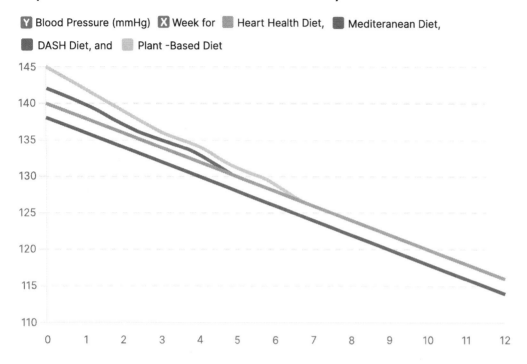

The Heart Health Diet

A highly recommended approach to maintaining cardiovascular health is the Heart Health Diet. This diet focuses on foods known to support heart function and reduce the risk of heart disease. It emphasizes a balance of fruits, vegetables, whole grains, lean proteins, and healthy fats. Research has shown that adhering to this diet can significantly lower cholesterol levels and blood pressure, leading to a reduced risk of heart disease.

Nutrition Patterns Highlight: Whole grains, fruits, vegetables, low-fat dairy, nuts, fish, poultry, and legumes; low in sodium, red meat, and added sugars.
The Aim: Improve heart function, reduce cholesterol and blood pressure, prevent heart disease, and promote overall cardiovascular health.

The Mediterranean Diet

One of the most well-documented success stories is the Mediterranean diet. Individuals in Mediterranean countries like Greece and Italy have lower rates of heart disease, which researchers attribute to their diet. This diet emphasizes fruits, vegetables, whole grains, fish, and healthy fats. Studies have shown that following this diet can reduce the risk of heart disease by up to 30%.

Nutrition Patterns Highlight: Primarily plant- based: high intake of vegetables, fruits, whole grains,beans,nuts and seeds,herbs and spices. high intake of Olive oil and Fish. Low intake of dairy, poultry and red meat.

The Aim: Weight loss, heart and brain health, cancer prevention and diabetes control and prevention.

The DASH Diet

The DASH (Dietary Approaches to Stop Hypertension) diet is another excellent example. Designed to combat high blood pressure, this diet is rich in fruits, vegetables, whole grains, nuts, fish, poultry and low-fat dairy. While being low in saturated fat, cholesterol, and sodium. Participants in studies following the DASH diet have seen significant reductions in blood pressure and improvements in overall heart health.

Nutrition Patterns Highlight: Whole grains, fruits, vegetables, low-fat dairy,nuts, fish,poultry and legumes. Low in sodium,red meat and sugar.

The Aim: Lowering blood pressure, lowering LDL

Plant-Based Diet

Increasingly, people are turning to plant-based diets to improve heart health. A study from the Journal of the American College of Cardiology found that those who follow a plant-based diet have a 16% lower risk of heart disease. Notable individuals like former President Bill Clinton have famously adopted a plant-based diet after experiencing heart problems, leading to significant health improvements.

Nutrition Patterns Highlight: Whole grains, fruits, vegetables,nuts and legumes. No animal products, eggs, fish, meats and poultry.

The Aim: Improving overall health preventing chronic disease and possible weight loss

The Bottom Line

The impact of diet on heart health is undeniable. By making informed dietary choices, you can significantly reduce the risk of heart disease and improve the overall health. Emphasizing fruits, vegetables, whole grains, healthy fats, and lean proteins while avoiding high levels of saturated fats, sugar, and processed foods can lead to a healthier heart and a longer, more vibrant life.

Remember, it's never too late to start making heart-healthy changes. Small, consistent adjustments to your diet can lead to significant improvements in your cardiovascular health over time.

The Purpose of This Book

This cookbook is designed for anyone who wants to embrace a heart-healthy lifestyle, whether you're a beginner or someone looking to enhance your current heart health regimen. Of course, the intention is not to complicate healthy eating for the heart, but to make a concise and quite actionable plan for improvement. Here's what you can expect:

90-Day Meal Plan

A comprehensive meal plan designed to guide you through three months of heart-healthy eating. This plan is structured to gradually introduce you to new foods and recipes, making the transition smooth and sustainable.

Delicious and Simple Recipes

A collection of recipes that are not only good for your heart but also easy to prepare and delicious. Each recipe is crafted with the beginner cook in mind, ensuring that you can create tasty meals without spending hours in the kitchen.

Educational Insights

Throughout the book, you'll find helpful tips and information about heart health, nutrition, and cooking techniques. These insights are designed to empower you with the knowledge you need to make informed choices.

Practical Guidance

From grocery shopping tips to meal prepping advice, this book provides practical guidance to help you integrate heart-healthy eating into your daily routine seamlessly.

Your Journey to Better Heart Health

Deciding to improve your heart health is one of the most inspirational steps and transformative decisions. It will not only provide you with the recipes of the tasty meal, but will also act as the manual on how to become a healthier person. When preparing meals for yourself or your family, you will find that it is enriching and delightful to feed your heart as well.

Anything that is done in modifying the diet is a step in the right direction in preventing poor heart health. It is my hope that this book will encourage you to make positive changes in your dietary habits when it comes to your heart with confidence and zeal. To beautiful dishes and healthy hearts, cheers!

Milanja Books

01

Understanding Heart-Healthy Eating

Risk factors

Factors like cholesterol, blood pressure, and other aspects relating to heart health are critical to the overall cardiovascular health and should, therefore, be well understood. All these factors are very important in the functioning of our cardiovascular system, and can be greatly influenced by things we eat and do.

Risk factors that's possible to manage

1. Cholesterol

Cholesterol is a fat-like substance which circulates in our bloodstream and is also made by the liver. This is a white waxy substance present in cell membranes, some hormones and bile acids. It is also important to understand that cholesterol levels depend on several factors such as genes, diet, weight, and activity. It turns out that there are two categories of cholesterol, high-density lipoprotein, or HDL—known as the 'good' cholesterol—and low–density lipoprotein, also known as the 'bad' cholesterol (LDL).

High-density lipoprotein (HDL), often called "good" cholesterol, plays a crucial role in removing "bad" cholesterol from the body. Therefore, higher levels of HDL are generally better for your health.

- **For Women:** "HDL levels below 50 mg/dl are considered risk factors for heart disease."

- **For Men:** "HDL levels below 40 mg/dl are considered risk factors for heart disease."

You can increase your HDL levels through aerobic exercise, losing weight, and avoiding tobacco products. If your HDL levels do not significantly increase despite these efforts, don't be discouraged. Low HDL levels might be influenced by genetics.

Low-density lipoproteins (LDL), are often referred to as "bad" cholesterol. Low-density lipoprotein also known as LDL transports cholesterol from the liver to other organs in the body, where it can be added to the walls of blood vessels. These vessels can accumulate cholesterol when their levels are high, resulting to blocked. While talking about problems with cholesterol, it is very common to mention triglyceride as well. Triglycerides are fats in their largest part, which enters the blood in the process of digestion of food products. Further, it is synthesized in the body with the help of foods rich in calories and deposited within the fat cells of the body. High content triglycerides may be caused by alcohol consumption or large amounts of sugar.

Be aware! Elevated triglyceride levels (150 or higher) combined with low HDL levels significantly increase the risk of heart disease.

Did you know? It is even possible to have high cholesterol levels, when there are no signs of the disease yet. In this case, please visit a doctor or nurse for advice on the frequency you should check your cholesterol levels.

2. Blood pressure

The pressure on the walls of the arteries from the inside is called blood pressure. Blood pressure is characterized by two numbers:

- **The first (upper)** means systolic pressure. It characterizes the pressure on the walls of blood vessels from within, when the heart beats.
- **The second (lower)** means diastolic pressure. It characterizes the pressure when the heart is at rest.

When the pressure inside the arteries is increased, the heart must pump more intensely to push blood through the blood vessels vessels. If high blood pressure (hypertension) is not treated, then the heart muscle will increase, and its performance will decrease.

Be aware! Blood pressure is considered normal if the top number is less than 120, and the lower one the number is less than 80.

3. Weight

Obesity raises the pressure on the heart, however, this danger can also be prevented by following a proper diet and performing regular workouts to uphold a healthy weight.

4 Weight Maintenance Components:

A healthy diet is one of the key determinants of the health of an individual since it determines the kind of nutrients that the body will be able to get. Meals containing high levels of saturated fats may lead to high cholesterol levels, thus leading to the incidence of coronary artery disease. These are associated with high sodium consumption, as it helps in retaining fluids in the body and irregular heartbeat due to either high or low potassium levels.

Avoiding foods containing a lot of **fats and sweets**

Practice **portion control** by not filing your tummy at every sight of food but wait until you are hungry or have a genuine reason to eat.

Aerobic exercise plays a role in maintaining Ideal weight, cholesterol levels, stress, blood pressure, Heart & Circulatory system strengthening Endurance, preventing the formation of thrombus in arteries, mental & emotional health enhancement, blood fat reduction, lesser appetite and many other benefits like muscle toning.

Did you know? Every extra pound of weight forces the heart to work harder, pushing blood further through the blood vessels.

4. Tabak

Smokers are 2-4 times more likely to develop heart disease compared to non-smokers and are 10 times more prone to peripheral arterial disease. Additionally, smokers face a higher risk of heart attack, stroke, circulatory disorders, cancer, and lung diseases.
Cigarette smoke contains approximately 7,000 chemicals substances. More than 70 of them are known to cause cancer. Tobacco products include cigarettes, electronic systems nicotine delivery (ENDS, including electronic cigarettes), cigars, smokeless tobacco (chewing tobacco or tobacco paste),hookahs, pipes, rolled cigarettes, as well as oral nicotine products.
Tobacco use is especially dangerous for blood vessels, in particular, arteries. It can lead to atherosclerosis, then there are deposits of plaque (a fatty substance found in blood). Over time, these deposits harden and narrow the gaps in blood vessels, in particular arteries. Smoking also makes blood vessels, including arteries, "sticky." There are obstructions to blood flow, which means that blood circulation is difficult. Side effects of tobacco use may require stenting, surgical intervention for coronary artery bypass surgery, or both and others to keep the lumens of the blood vessels open vessels, including arteries.Tobacco use can also lead to a heart attack or stroke.

Tobacco use dangers:

- Causes heart disease and stroke

- Increases heart rate

- Increases blood pressure

- Reduces the content of "good" (high density) cholesterol

- May cause cardiac arrhythmia

- Increases the load on the heart (creates additional strain on damaged or weakened blood vessels, including arteries)

- May affect the effectiveness of medications taken for heart diseases

- Causes heartburn and peptic ulcers

- May slow recovery after surgery.

A damaged heart must cope with the harmful effect of tobacco. If you quit smoking and avoid passive exposure smoking, this may help restore normal functioning hearts and damaged blood vessels, and also reduce risk of heart disease.

Warning! Don't smoke if you have diabetes. Smoking at two times the risk of heart disease. (Source: National educational program on diabetes)

Did you know? Second-hand smoke vapor from electronic cigarettes is also unsafe. IN vapors of electronic cigarettes contains many of those same residual chemical substances as in cigarettes smoke, including: heavy metals such as tin, nickel and chrome nicotine toxic substances such such as benzene, formaldehyde,lead and toluene.E-cigarette vapor consist of more closely spaced tiny particles (more than concentrated) than tobacco cigarette smoke.These tiny particles can get into people's lungs putting them at high risk shortness of breath and lung damage.

Source: Minister US health

5.Alcohol

Several previous studies have suggested that alcohol consumption is related with heart disease. The risk of developing an enlarged heart and heart failure may also rise when alcohol is consumed moderately or in large amounts and for a long period of time. Problem drinking can result in raised blood pressure; raised triglycerides and even raised calorie intake. Discuss your alcohol consumption status with the Health assistant who is treating you.

6.Stress

Strong emotions can cause your body to produce more adrenaline, a hormone that speeds up heart rate and increases blood pressure. Voltage causes small arteries in the body to become less, and may temporarily increase cholesterol levels in blood. How you react to stress will affect your body and emotional state. Stress you can try to control by avoiding situations that cause it.In a stressful situation, you should take more care of yourself.

Take deep breaths and exhale slowly. Don't drive myself. Don't drive during rush hours and don't go shopping during crowded shops. Set aside time for doing nothing or whatever you like. Look after yourself. To cope with stress, join a relaxation group, or try a massage.

7. Diabetes

Diabetes is also a risk factor to heart diseases since it affects the blood vessels. If diabetes is not managed, high blood glucose can increase triglyceride cholesterol thereby causing peripheral arterial disease.

Diabetes patients are 2-4 times likely to suffer from heart disease or stroke than individuals without diabetes. Statistics from the National Diabetes Education Program indicate that about 65 percent of diabetes-related deaths are due to heart disease or stroke.

In women's case, diabetes is a more critical risk factor than in men and showed that several diseases such as heart disease were more prevalent among women
.

Diabetes is a chronic disease, which means cannot be cured, but it can be controlled to a certain extent. Thus, it is vital to maintain blood glucose and lipid profiles, manage blood pressure, be physically active, maintain a normal weight, adhere to a healthy diet, and abstain from smoking to prevent heart diseases and stroke.

Be aware! You should maintain hemoglobin levels A1c below 7 percent. Discuss with your doctor or nurse, what fasting blood glucose level should be with you.

Tip: Do not smoke if you have diabetes. Smoking doubles the risk of developing heart disease.

Risk factors that's not possible to manage

1. Age

In general, the risk of coronary artery disease increases with age. The older we grow, the more plaque will form in our arteries. It is also found that the higher the level of these plaques, then there is more possibility that these plaques could rupture and lead to the formation of blood clots. It can also lead to heart attack or some sort of reduced blood flow to the heart region.

2. Gender

The given fact shows that for men heart disease can develop at an earlier age than for women. But, after menopause the risk factor of the heart diseases in women is on the gradual rise and finally becomes parallel to that of the man. Estrogen is known to provide some protection against the development of atherosclerosis in the human body. Thereby Atherosclerosis (hardening of the arteries) develops more slowly in women than in men.

3. Genetic

A history of heart disease in immediate family members at a young age is a sign that caution may be necessary.
It includes: Heart attacks, bypass surgery, angioplasty, or sudden cardiac death:

- in fathers or brothers - before age 55
- in mothers or sisters -before age 65

If you have a genetic predisposition to heart disease, it is crucial to be mindful of other risk factors, such as high cholesterol. Your doctor may recommend testing your cholesterol levels and performing a blood profile to assess your risk further.

Set realistic goals to reduce your risk factors for heart disease.

Risk	Your health profile	My target
High blood pressure	Blood pressure range: _____	• Low then 120/80
High Cholesterol	Date: _____ Low density lipoproteins: _____ High density lipoproteins: _____ Triglycerides: _____	• LDL 100 mg/dL or lower • HDL: Men 40 mg/dL or higher • HDL: Women 50 mg/dL or higher • Triglycerides below 150 mg/dL
Smoking	Have you used tobacco products during the last year? _____	• Stop smoking
Sport exercises	My last program? _____ _____	• Regular exercise such as Pilates, walking, cycling. Not less than 30 min. every or almost every day
Weight	Am I overweight? _____ My weight _____	• Lose weight by _____
Stress	Do you think that you are under stress that you cannot manage? _____	• Identify the nature of stress and cope with it in healthy ways, such as exercise or relaxation.
Diabetes	Date: _____ Glucose: _____ Glycated hemoglobin A1c: _____	• Discuss with your healthcare team what your blood glucose levels should be on fasting. • Glucose hemoglobin A1c below 7%

Key Dietary Components for Heart Health

 1. Fruits and Vegetables

Fruits and Vegetables are good sources of vitamins and minerals. They are very calorie-free and fiber-full, so they should definitely be included in anyone's diet plan. Such plant based foods have nutrients that have the potential of reducing the outbreaks of heart diseases. Furthermore, including fruits and vegetables during meal preparations will assist one to cut down on high calorie foods including meats, cheese and snacks.

It is easy to increase the intake of vegetables and fruits in your diet. Use pre-washed and cut vegetables to make them easily accessible for snacking when placed in the refrigerator. Put a bowl of fruit in your kitchen to ensure that you eat healthy food instead of packaged snacks. Select dishes where vegetables or fruits are the main components of the dish for example fried vegetables or fruit based salads.

Good to know: "Heart" vitamins like A, C, E and B are very good for the heart.

Fruits and vegetables to choose:

- Fresh or frozen vegetables and fruits,
- Low-sodium canned vegetables,
- Canned fruit packed in 100% juice or water,
- Leafy green vegetables, Edamame, Cabbage, Okra, Tomatos, Avocados, Carrots
- Berries, blueberries, blackberries, Red grapes, Apples, Mangos, Pomegranate, Cherries, Kiwi

Fruits and vegetables to limit:

- Vegetables with creamy sauces,
- Coconut,
- Fried or breaded vegetables,
- Canned fruit packed in heavy syrup
- Frozen fruit with sugar added

Did you know? A study published in the American Heart Association journal found that individuals who consumed at least five servings of fruits and vegetables daily had a 20% lower risk of heart disease compared to those who ate fewer servings.

 ## 2. Whole Grains

Daily intake of at least three servings of whole grain foods can lower the chances of heart disease by as much as thirty percent lower than that of individuals who rarely consume whole grain foods. Whole grains are indispensable in the diet to improve cardiovascular health, as they contain all three components of the grain's original parts: the bran, the germ, and the endosperm; in fact, whole grains are healthy foods with antioxidants, fiber and nutrients. Out of these beneficial components, fiber stands out as the most effective in battling heart diseases. In other words, "A 2022 systematic review and meta-analysis published in BMC Medicine has shown that consuming whole grain foods can be protective against risk of heart disease." Also in 2019 a study on Nutrients indicates that an increased fiber intake reduces cholesterol, blood pressure and atheroma formation.

Moreover, data in Circulation Research suggest that dietary fiber reduces inflammation through its effect on gut microbiota to decrease inflammation systemically which is associated with risk of cardiovascular disease, hypertension or atherosclerosis.

Whole grains also contain certain chemical compounds from plants called phytochemicals that have antioxidant and anti-inflammatory properties that help in preventing chronic illnesses like heart diseases. These, one would say are some of the loads of heart health benefits one can derive from consuming mouth-watering foods.

Here are some whole-grain foods:

- Amaranth
- Barley
- Brown rice
- Buckwheat
- Bulgur
- Corn
- Farro
- Millet
- Oatmeal
- Oats (rolled or steel cut)
- Popcorn
- Quinoa
- Sorghum
- Spelt
- Teff
- Whole-wheat bread
- Whole-grain pasta
- Wild rice

Did you know? The Nurses' Health Study, which followed over 75,000 women for 10 years, reported that those who consumed whole grains regularly had a 25% lower risk of heart disease.

 3. Fats

Fats are classified as the nutrient substance and it is important that the body receives fat in order to perform its functions. However, if the intake of fat is too much, then it raises the content cholesterol within blood and the chances of getting heart diseases will be raised.

The first measure to take care when trying to minimize your possibilities of having heart problems is to reduce saturated fats, cholesterol and the hydrogenated fats. Reduced dietary fat in particular assists in reduction of total cholesterol counts and therefore provides a longer and healthier livelihood. While natural and healthy foods such as fruits and vegetables are recommended in the diet, foods rich in fats are associated with obesity, heart diseases, and cancer.

In fact: Unsaturated fats, such as those found in olive oil and avocados, can help reduce bad cholesterol levels (LDL) and increase good cholesterol levels (HDL).

Bad Fats:

Saturated fats are found in animal products such as butter, cheese, whole milk, ice cream and fatty meat. They are also found in some food plant origin such as coconut, palm and palm kernel oil. **Saturated and hydrogenated fats fatty acids increase blood cholesterol levels more so than any other food.**

Hydrogenated fats Hydrogenated fatty acids (hydrogenated fats) are obtained using the chemical process of hydrogenation. Hydrogenated fats may increase the content of low-density lipoproteins and contribute to heart disease.Shortening, partially hydrogenated vegetable oil and hydrogenated vegetable oil are examples of hydrogenated fats. These fats are often used when preparing dishes in many restaurants and businesses.

Note: Hydrogenated fats are found naturally in some foods such as meat or milk.)

Tip: Always read ingredient labels. Buy foods that contain recommended fat, e.g. rapeseed or soybean oil. Avoid buying products containing shortening, partially hydrogenated or hydrogenated vegetable oil. Choose products containing hydrogenated fats close to zero.

Good Fats:

Polyunsaturated fats include corn, safflower, sunflower, soybean, cottonseed, and sesame oils. Polyunsaturated fats can help reduce bad cholesterol levels (LDL) and may increase good cholesterol levels (HDL) if used instead of saturated fats.

Monounsaturated fats The main sources of monounsaturated fats include olive oil, peanut oils and rapeseed oil. Avocados and most types of nuts also contain high amounts of monounsaturated fats. It is especially important to point out that increased consumption of monounsaturated fats within the diet may be beneficial and reduce total cholesterol and LDL cholesterol concentrations generally referred to as "bad" cholesterol.

Did you know? The Mediterranean diet, rich in olive oil, nuts, and fish, has been linked to a 30% reduction in the risk of heart disease, as shown in a study published in the New England Journal of Medicine.

4. Lean Proteins

According to several researchers' works, using lean meats instead of fatty ones and increasing fish, beans, poultry, nuts, and low-fat dairy foods consumption may reduce the risk of Heart Disease. Proteins in these foods have the potentiality to reduce cholesterol and blood pressure levels as well as assist in keeping off extra calories. So if you can choose these proteins instead of high-fat meats, you stand a better chance of not falling victim to heart attack or stroke.

Scientific publications such as "Circulation" have provided evidence that higher amounts of red meat consumption raise the chance of developing coronary heart disease. To reduce that risk, you need to move to lower risk protein sources.

Increasing the amount of fish and nuts consumed is one of the ways that has been proven to reduce the risk of heart disease. While one serving per day of nuts was associated with a 30 percent reduction in heart disease risk, one serving per day of red meat was associated with an increased risk of heart disease by the same percent.

In the same way, a single portion of fish each day reduced risk by 24 percent, poultry and low fat dairy products also decreased risk by 19% and 13% respectively.

Did you know? Research from the Harvard School of Public Health found that replacing red meat with plant-based proteins like beans and legumes can lower the risk of heart disease by 14%.

Here are some Lean Proteins:

White-fleshed fish: All the white-fleshed fish are moderately lean in terms of fat content, and are ideal sources of protein. Some types of white fish which are very low in fat include cod, haddock, grouper, halibut, tilapia and bass. It is rich in protein and contains very low fat and calories, although other fishes like salmon, have better amounts of omega 3 fatty acids.

Frozen shrimp: Frozen unbreaded shrimp are a convenient option. A 3 oz (85 g) serving has 110 calories, 22 g of protein, and 2 g of fat.

Skinless white poultry meat: A 3.5 oz (100 g) serving of cooked chicken or turkey breast has around 30 g of protein.

Lean beef: Of ground beef, try to get the leanest possible – 90% is recommended. A 4 oz (113 g) cooked hamburger patty containing 95 % ground beef has calories of 155, 5g. It contains 6g of total fat, 2. 4 g of which is saturated fat and 24g of protein. Lean beef is known as "loin" and "round", and they contain a high protein content and a very high content of B vitamins, zinc, and selenium.

Pork loin: Lean cuts include pork tenderloin, pork (loin) chops, and pork top loin or sirloin roasts. Pork tenderloin, the leanest cut, has 109 calories, 21 g of protein, and about 2.7 g of fat per 3.5 oz (100 g) cooked serving. Be sure to cut off excess fat on the meat if you're trying to limit fat and calories.

Beans, peas, and lentils: Dry beans, peas, and lentils, also called pulses, are a subgroup of legumes. They average 20-25 Trusted Source of protein per 1/2 cup (100 g) cooked serving, depending on the type Trusted Source.

Did you know? A 2021 review Trusted Source explains that eating legumes can have a positive effect on a variety of health markers, including reducing cholesterol, improving the body's glucose management, protecting blood vessels, and reducing inflammation.

Powdered peanut butter: The naturally occurring oil in peanut butter is heart-healthy but the calories can really add up. A standard serving of around 3.5 oz (100 g) of regular peanut butter has 500-600 calories, 50 g of fat, with 24 g of protein included. A reduced calorie variant of peanut butter is the unsweetened powdered peanut butter. The same serving contains 375 calories and 8 grams of fat, but 33 grams of protein.

Plain Greek yogurt: It is advised to use plain, non-fat or low-fat Greek yogurt as they contain twice the amount of protein per serving as regular yogurt and are low in sugar.

Low fat milk: A 1-cup serving of low fat milk with 1% milk fat has 8 g of protein, 2 g of fat, and 105 calories. In comparison, a serving of whole milk with 3.25% milk fat has the same amount of protein but 146 calories and about 8 g of fat.

Low fat cottage cheese: One cup (226 g) of low fat (2% milk fat) cottage cheese has 163 calories, 2.5 g of fat, and 28 g of protein.

Tofu: A 3 oz (85 g) serving of tofu has 71 calories, 3.5 g of fat, and 9 g of protein Trusted Source, including sufficient amounts of all the essential amino acids.

Edamame: A cup (160 grams) of cooked edamame provides around 18.5 grams of protein.

Egg whites: One egg white contains less than 0.5 g of fat but 3.6 g of protein, which is a little less than half of the protein in a whole egg. Thus, even whole eggs are allowed at least in limited measures while observing a diet to promote the health of your heart and in case you are looking for an even more lightweight solution you can use only whites.

Chickpea: A 1-cup (164-gram) serving provides about 14.5 grams of protein, which is comparable to the protein content of similar foods like black beans and lentils.

How Much Protein Do You Need?Determining the right amount of heart-healthy protein for your diet is crucial for maintaining overall health. Typically, 10–30 percent of your daily calories should come from protein. The Recommended Dietary Allowance (RDA) for protein is:

- **Women (ages 19+):** 46 grams per day

- **Men (ages 19+):** 56 grams per day

For instance, an adult can get his daily protein intake in a day by taking a proportion of these foods:

- **1 cup of milk:** 8 grams of protein.

- **6 ounces of salmon:** 34 grams of protein.

- **1 cup of dried beans:** 16 grams of protein

 5. Low Sodium

Salt, which is made up of sodium, is an important mineral that keeps fluids in the correct balance in your bloodstream. However, too much sodium leads to your vessels retaining more water. High blood pressure, itself thought to be a major cause of heart failure, can become more pronounced, as it's experienced by many heart-failure patients. That, in turn, can lead to more swelling, weight gain, fluid retention and bloating caused by the fact that the heart can't pump as efficiently as it used to before heart-failure symptoms arose.

If you want to treat your condition well, you have to keep your sodium levels on the right track so that you don't have too much or too little — just the right amount.

In fact: the World Health Organization recommends a maximum adult salt intake of 5 g/day (2 g sodium/day), while The American Heart Association recommends a total sodium intake between 2.3 g/day (equivalent to 5.7 g salt/day) to 1.5 g/day (equivalent to 3.75 g salt/day) in high risk-patients for CVD.

Tips to reduce salt :

- Try using herbs and seasonings that do not contain salt.

- Remove the salt shaker from the table.

- Reduce the amount of salt when cooking or cook without salt.

- Reduce the amount of salt used for seasonings.

- Reduce your consumption of prepared foods.

Did you know? The DASH (Dietary Approaches to Stop Hypertension) diet, which emphasizes low sodium intake, has been proven to lower blood pressure and reduce the risk of heart disease.

Tips on grocery shopping and meal prepping.

The heart is one of the most important organs in the body, and diet is a substantial factor in heart health. Grocery shopping and meal prepping are some of the strategies that you can use to maintain a proper diet and be able to take foods that are recommendable for the heart. This overview includes general guidelines and plans for consuming healthy foods while grocery shopping and for planning meals to help establish proper cardiovascular function.

Here are some tips for making a good choice:

Don't be hungry: going to the grocery shop while hungry only increases the chance to buy unnecessary or needed products and also grab some chips or candies. Have a snack before shopping. It can be apple and sandwich or non-fat Greek yogurt.

Plan Ahead: For your shopping, make sure that you have the weekly menus and so make a list of everything you will require before going shopping. It will make you avoid so many impulse purchases and will help you spend less money on groceries.

Make a List: Before preparing your shopping list, check your pantry, cupboards, refrigerator and the freezer to eliminate any product that you may have purchased more than once. It is helpful to know how the store looks and organized. Your grocery list can also be divided by categories such as fruits and vegetables, fat free dairy products, lean proteins, whole grain & etc.

Shop the Perimeter: While searching for a healthier option in the grocery store, always look at the aisles on the outside of the store. These peripheral sectors commonly consist of unprocessed foods such as fruits, vegetables, whole grain products, lean meats, and nonfat dairy foods. However, the interior aisles are generally filled with lots of processed foods. For efficiency during shopping, request for a store map and set your route. It is recommended not to wander too much in the center aisles except buying necessary items like brown rice, wheat pasta, oatmeal, quinoa and beans. Thus, this strategy assists you in being more effective in the choices you make for the heart.

Choose Whole Grains: Look for the term "whole.'" Make sure that the food or product contains a whole grain in the first place in the list of ingredients. Buy specific whole grain products such as sorghum, brown rice, oats, bread, and pasta.

Go lean: While considering proteins, check for the label 'lean' and endeavor to use lean meats like top sirloin, flank steak and tenderloin for red meats and skinless chicken breasts for poultry. If it is possible to choose the canned fish or the chicken which are canned in water and have labeling of "no added salt" or "lower sodium".

No added sugar or salt: Make sure that you pick frozen vegetables without any sauces, seasonings, or added salt. Canned vegetables and beans are usually the most common high saturated product containing sodium so unless you wish to eat them you should first rinse them or then drain them to remove excess water. When buying canned fruit, it is suggested to pick the one that is packed in water, with natural juices, or those that have the label of "no added sugar", rather than the canned sugar-syrupy kind, which are made from sugared, syrupy or sweetened sweet fruit for the frozen fruits do not include fruits cooked with sugar, syrups or sweeteners.

Did you know? Research from the American Heart Association highlighted that people who consume high amounts of added sugars have a 38% higher risk of dying from cardiovascular disease.

Be aware! Processed foods often contain high levels of sodium, unhealthy fats, and sugars, and lack essential nutrients, leading to poor heart health.

Low-fat: Pick low-fat 1% or fat-free milk and buttermilk for your dairy needs. Go for low-fat cheese to cut down on saturated fats that can jack up your cholesterol. Skip skim milk yogurt - non-fat Greek yogurt packs more protein punch or Cottage cheese. Grab the low-fat kind to boost your diet's health factor. Milk alternatives, it's a good choice. Stick to unsweetened soy, oat, or hemp milk with added calcium for a nutrient boost. These choices have a big influence on your overall health so pick !

Healthy Fats: Pick oils that aren't saturated: Canola, olive, and peanut oils are the heavy hitters. Go for soft or liquid margarines that don't contain any hydrogenated oils , light or non fat salad dressings .Don't forget seedless and unsalted dry roasted nuts. Are you in the mood for sprucing up your meal and improving your heart health? Prepare a low salt dressing full of flavor by using vinegar, and add olive oil. There is no doubt your belly will be glad too!

Read Labels: Discover the art of becoming a better Nutrition Facts food label reader. To include more heart healthy foods in your diet plan, start by cutting back on trans- fatty acid and saturated fat intake, and increasing fiber intake.

Tip: Keep an eye on Saturated Fat, Trans Fat and Cholesterol and Sodium.

Serving size: Serving size shows amount of food in one serving and quantity servings in one package.

Calories: This is a measure of the energy released by food. Try to choose products that are a source of less one third of calories.

Saturated fats: Saturated fats increase LDL cholesterol levels (so-called "bad" cholesterol). Saturated fats, found in red meat and full-fat dairy products. To save heart health, reduce the amount of consumption of saturated fats.

Trans fats: Trans fats can increase LDL cholesterol levels, reduce HDL cholesterol level (the so-called "good" cholesterol) and promote heart disease diseases. Trans fats found in many processed and fried foods. Eat as Less trans fats as possible. Avoid products that contain "partially hydrogenated vegetable oils.

Cholesterol: Foods high in cholesterol include meat, fish, eggs, cheese, butter and other animal related products.

Sodium: Sodium (table salt) is essential for normal organ function and supports fluid balance in the body. Superfluous amounts of sodium can lead to increased blood pressure. One teaspoon of table salt contains 2400 mg of sodium. This is the greatest amount of sodium most people need every day.

Product A

Nutrition Facts

Per burger (85g)

Calories 250

Amount	% Daily Value*
Total Fat 18g	28%
Saturated Fat 7g	38%
Trans Fat 0.5g	
Cholesterol 55 mg	
Sodium 330 mg	14%
Total Carbohydrate 1 g	1%
Dietary Fiber 0g	0%
Sugars 5g	
Protein 12 mg	
Vitamin A	4%
Calcium	2%

Product B

Nutrition Facts

Per burger (85g)

Calories 150

Amount	% Daily Value*
Total Fat 7g	17%
Saturated Fat 3g	17%
Trans Fat 0.5g	
Cholesterol 33 mg	
Sodium 200 mg	8%
Total Carbohydrate 1 g	1%
Dietary Fiber 0 g	0%
Sugars 0 g	
Protein 14 mg	
Vitamin A	4%
Calcium	2%

Total carbohydrates: Carbohydrates are a source of body energy. Excessive amounts of carbohydrates can increase blood glucose levels. The effect of carbohydrates on the level of glucose in a person's blood individually.

Cellulose: This is the part of food that is not broken down by the progress of digestion. As it passes through the body "undigested", then it plays an important role in maintaining the digestive system in active working condition.

Total sugars: Total sugars include the amount of all natural sugars such as lactose (sugar in milk) or fructose (sugar in fruits), and all added sugars.

Added sugars. This is the portion of total sugar that is added when cooking.

Protein: Protein is important for the healing process, growth muscle mass, and strengthening the immune system.

02

90-Day Meal Plan

Plan a Heart-Healthy Week: Simple Steps for Better Health

One of the most important factors that can help stick to a healthy meal plan is the proper planning of the meals. Begin with the goal to plan your menus a week in advance. Choose your recipes and make a shopping list, including the exact amounts of every ingredient you will require. Also, make sure that your list contains healthy snacks and ingredients for breakfast, lunch, and dinner recipes. This helps prevent the common scenario of going to the kitchen only to find that there is nothing to eat because the shelves are stocked with healthy foods encouraging healthy eating habits.

When grocery shopping, people always end up buying more than what they need hence, food wastes and more spending. Most supermarkets have corrected this problem by coming up with bulk bins for things like grains, beans, and seeds, nuts and spices, and dried fruits so that people can buy only the quantities that they require.

When planning for the week's meal, prepare your kitchen in a way that your equipment is within reach and all equipment is in place. Carefully read through each recipe before starting to record the prep time, which is the time required for cutting and preparing the ingredients, and the cook time, which is the time taken to cook the dish.

Some simple strategies will allow you, as well as your family, to improve your diet, reduce the risk of further deterioration of cardiovascular disease, and economize on food expenses.

Weekly meal plans

This cookbook provides comprehensive meal plans for two months. The first month focuses on a 1,200-calorie meal plan, ideal for those recently diagnosed with a heart condition. The second month offers a 1,500-calorie meal plan to help maintain the progress achieved. Additionally, there is a bonus one-week 2,000-calorie meal plan designed to promote a healthy heart.

After completing these plans, you can create your own weekly meal plans using the recipes in this book and continue enjoying a healthy heart.

Further is a breakdown of meals for a month with an emphasis on 1200 calorie daily diet for a heart healthy lifestyle.

Week 1

	Breakfas	Lunch	Dinner	Snack
Monday	Oatmeal with berries	Grilled chicken salad	Baked salmon with steamed veggies	Apple slices with almond butter
Tuesday	Greek yogurt with honey &nuts	Quinoa salad with chickpeas	Turkey stir-fry with brown rice	Carrot sticks with hummus
Wednesday	Whole grain toast with avocado	Lentil soup with whole grain roll	Grilled shrimp with mixed greens	Handful of mixed nuts
Thursday	Smoothie with spinach and banana	Tuna salad with whole grain crackers	Stuffed bell peppers	Orange slices
Friday	Scrambled eggs with spinach	Chicken wrap with veggies	Baked cod with sweet potato	Celery sticks with peanut butter
Saturday	Cottage cheese with pineapple	Veggie burger on whole grain bun	Beef and broccoli stir-fry	Greek yogurt with berries
Sunday	Whole grain cereal with milk	Tomato and mozzarella salad	Grilled chicken with quinoa	Apple

Week 2

	Breakfas	Lunch	Dinner	Snack
Monday	Oatmeal with sliced banana	Garbanzo Bean Salad with Pitas	Grilled tilapia with asparagus	Handful of almonds
Tuesday	Smoothie with berries and chia	Turkey and avocado sandwich	Quinoa stuffed bell peppers	Baby carrots with hummus
Wednesday	Greek yogurt with granola	Veggie soup with whole grain bread	Chicken and vegetable stir-fry	Cottage cheese with peach slices
Thursday	Whole grain toast with almond butter	Grilled chicken Caesar salad	Shrimp and quinoa bowl	Apple slices with peanut butter
Friday	Egg White Frittata	Tuna and mixed greens salad	Baked salmon with brown rice	Celery sticks with almond butter
Saturday	Cottage cheese with blueberries	Quinoa and black bean salad	Turkey meatballs with zucchini	Greek yogurt with honey
Sunday	Whole grain cereal with berries	Chicken wrap with veggies	Grilled steak with green beans	Orange slices

Week 3

	Breakfas	Lunch	Dinner	Snack
Monday	Oatmeal with apple slices	Chickpea salad with veggies	Grilled chicken with sweet potato	Handful of walnuts
Tuesday	Smoothie with mango and spinach	Turkey salad with mixed greens	Grilled cod with quinoa	Carrot sticks with hummus
Wednesday	Greek yogurt with nuts	Lentil soup with whole grain bread	Baked salmon with broccoli	Celery sticks with peanut butter
Thursday	Whole grain toast with peanut butter	Chicken and avocado wrap	Shrimp stir-fry with brown rice	Apple slices
Friday	Scrambled eggs with spinach	Tuna and avocado salad	Baked chicken with green beanso	Cottage cheese with pineapple
Saturday	Cottage cheese with raspberries	Quinoa salad with veggies	Beef stir-fry with vegetables	Greek yogurt with granola
Sunday	Whole grain cereal with milk	Caprese salad	Grilled turkey burger with salad	Handful of mixed nuts

Week 4

	Breakfas	Lunch	Dinner	Snack
Monday	Oatmeal with chia seeds	Spinach and chicken salad	Baked salmon with asparagus	Baby carrots with hummus
Tuesday	Smoothie with blueberries	Turkey and quinoa bowl	Grilled shrimp with brown rice	Apple slices with almond butter
Wednesday	Greek yogurt with honey and nuts	Veggie soup with whole grain bread	Chicken stir-fry with vegetables	Handful of almonds
Thursday	Whole grain toast with avocado	Tuna salad with mixed greens	Stuffed bell peppers	Cottage cheese with peach slices
Friday	Egg White Frittata	Quinoa and black bean salad	Grilled tilapia with green beans	Celery sticks with peanut butter
Saturday	Cottage cheese with strawberries	Turkey wrap with veggies	Baked chicken with quinoa	Greek yogurt with berries
Sunday	Whole grain cereal with milk	Chickpea and avocado salad	Beef and broccoli stir-fry	Orange slices

90 - Day Meal Plan

Here is a breakdown of meals for a 4 weeks, with an emphasis on 1500 calorie/day.

Week 1

	Breakfas	Lunch	Dinner	Snack
Monday	Oatmeal with berries and almonds	Grilled chicken salad with vinaigrette	Baked salmon with quinoa and spinach	Greek yogurt with honey and walnuts
Tuesday	Scrambled eggs with vegetables	Turkey and avocado wrap	Stir-fried tofu with vegetables	Apple slices with peanut butter
Wednesday	Smoothie with spinach and banana	Lentil soup with a side salad	Grilled chicken with brown rice & broccoli	Carrot sticks with hummus
Thursday	Greek yogurt with granola	Quinoa salad with chickpeas	Baked cod with sweet potato & green beans	Mixed nuts
Friday	Whole-grain cereal with skim milk	Tuna salad on whole-grain bread	Vegetable stir-fry with tofu	Cottage cheese with pineapple
Saturday	Whole-wheat pancakes with fruit	Chicken and vegetable soup	Spaghetti ,marinara & turkey meatballs	Celery sticks with almond butter
Sunday	Avocado toast with a poached egg	Black bean and corn salad	Grilled shrimp with quinoa & asparagus	Fresh fruit

Week 2

	Breakfas	Lunch	Dinner	Snack
Monday	Smoothie bowl with berries & seeds	Spinach & feta wrap	Baked chicken with wild rice & carrots	Cherry tomatoes with mozzarella
Tuesday	Oatmeal with chia seeds & bananas	Quinoa & black bean salad	Grilled salmon with steamed vegetables	Mixed berries
Wednesday	Greek yogurt with honey & flaxseed	Lentil & vegetable stewd	Shrimp stir-fry with brown rice	Apple slices with almond butter
Thursday	Whole-grain toast with avocado	Chicken Caesar salad (light dressing)	Baked tilapia with quinoa & broccoli	Greek yogurt with honey
Friday	Smoothie with s pinach & berriess	Turkey & veggie wrap	Vegetable pasta with marinara sauce	Hummus with whole-gr. crackers
Saturday	Scrambled eggs with vegetables	Chickpea salad with lemon dressing	Grilled turkey burger with sweet potato	Cottage cheese with pineapple
Sunday	Whole-grain waffles with fruit	Tuna & avocado salad	Grilled chicken with brown rice & green b...	Sliced cucumbers

Week 3

	Breakfas	Lunch	Dinner	Snack
Monday	Overnight oats with fruit	Chicken and vegetable stir-fry	Baked salmon, sweet potatoes & spinach	Mixed nuts
Tuesday	Greek yogurt with berries	Turkey & avocado wrap	Tofu and vegetable curry with brown	Carrot sticks with hummus
Wednesday	Smoothie with spinach & banana	Lentil soup with a side salad	Grilled chicken with quinoa & broccoli	Apple slices with peanut butter
Thursday	Oatmeal with almonds and honey	Quinoa salad with chickpeas	Baked cod with wild rice & green beans	Greek yogurt with honey
Friday	Whole-grain cereal with skim milk	Tuna salad on whole-grain bread	Vegetable stir-fry with tofu	Cottage cheese with pineapple
Saturday	Whole-wheat pancakes with fruit	Chicken and vegetable soup	Spaghetti marinara & turkey meatballs	Celery sticks with almond butter
Sunday	Avocado toast with a poached egg	Black bean & corn salad	Grilled shrimp with quinoa & asparagus	Fresh fruit

Week 4

	Breakfas	Lunch	Dinner	Snack
Monday	Smoothie bowl with berries & seeds	Spinach & feta wrap	Baked chicken with wild rice& carrots	Cherry tomatoes with mozzarella
Tuesday	Oatmeal with chia seeds and bananas	Quinoa & black bean salad	Grilled salmon with steamed vegetables	Mixed berries
Wednesday	Greek yogurt with honey & flaxseed	Lentil & vegetable stew	Shrimp stir-fry with brown rice	Apple slices with almond butter
Thursday	Whole-grain toast with avocado	Chicken Caesar salad (light dressing)	Baked tilapia with quinoa and broccoli	Greek yogurt with honey
Friday	Smoothie with spinach and berries	Turkey & veggie wrap	Vegetable pasta with marinara sauce	Hummus with whole-grain cr...
Saturday	Scrambled eggs with vegetables	Chickpea salad with lemon dressing	Grilled turkey burger with sweet potato	Cottage cheese with pineapple
Sunday	Whole-grain waffles with fruit	Tuna & avocado salad	Grilled chicken with brown rice & green b...	Sliced cucumbers with hummus

Bonus: *Here is a breakdown of meals for a 1 week, with an emphasis on 2000 calorie/day.*

Week 1

	Breakfas	Lunch	Dinner	Snack
Monday	Oatmeal with berries and almonds	Grilled chicken salad with vinaigrette	Baked salmon with quinoa and spinach	Greek yogurt with honey and walnuts
Tuesday	Egg White Frittata with w.g. toast	Turkey and avocado wrap	Stir-fried tofu with vegetables	Apple slices with peanut butter
Wednesday	Smoothie with s pinach and banana	Lentil soup with a side salad	Grilled chicken with brown rice & broccoli	Carrot sticks with hummus
Thursday	Greek yogurt with granola	Quinoa salad with chickpeas	Baked cod with sweet potato & green beans	Mixed nuts
Friday	Whole-grain cereal with skim milk	Tuna salad on whole-grain bread	Vegetable stir-fry with tofu	Cottage cheese with pineapple
Saturday	Whole-wheat pancakes with fruit	Chicken and vegetable soup	Spaghetti ,marinara & turkey meatballs	Celery sticks with almond butter
Sunday	Avocado toast with a poached egg	Black bean and corn salad	Grilled shrimp with quinoa & asparagus	Fresh fruit

03

Chapter

Breakfast
& Smoothies

Whole grain toasts with Avocado

Prep time
5 mins

Cook Time
5 mins

Servings
2 per.

Calorie
206 kcal/Toast

Ingredients:

- **2** slices of whole grain bread
- **1** ripe avocado
- **1** small tomato, sliced
- **1** radish, thinly sliced (optional)
- **1** tablespoon olive oil (optional)
- **1** teaspoon lemon juice
- **1/4** teaspoon salt & black pepper

Instructions:

1.
- Slice the tomato and radish thinly.
- Halve the avocado, remove the pit, and scoop the flesh into a bowl.
- Add the lemon juice, salt, and black pepper to the avocado. Mash until smooth but slightly chunky.

2.
- Toast the slices of whole grain bread to your desired level of crispiness.
- Spread the mashed avocado evenly over the toasted bread slices.
- Arrange the tomato and radish slices on top of the avocado.

3.
- Drizzle olive oil over the top of the assembled toast.
- Garnish with fresh cilantro or parsley if desired.

Whole grain toasts with poached egg

Prep time
5 mins

Cook Time
5 mins

Servings
2 per.

Calorie
255 kcal/Toast

Ingredients:

- Use the same ingredients like in Avocado Toast

- Instead radish, you can use a handful of fresh spinach leaves

- **2** large eggs

Instructions for Poaching Eggs:

- Fill a medium saucepan with about 3 inches of water. Bring it to a simmer over medium heat.

- Crack each egg into a small bowl or ramekin.

- Create a gentle whirlpool in the water with a spoon and carefully slide each egg into the center of the whirlpool. This helps the egg whites wrap around the yolks.

- Let the eggs cook for about 3-4 minutes for a runny yolk or longer if you prefer a firmer yolk.

- Remove the eggs with a slotted spoon and drain on a paper towel.

Instructions:

- Follow the same guidelines as those used for the Avocado toast, until section 2: "Spread the mashed avocado evenly over the toasted bread slices."

- Top each toast with fresh spinach leaves and diced tomatoes.

- Carefully place a poached egg on top of each toast.

- Drizzle olive oil over the top of the assembled toast.

- Garnish with fresh cilantro or parsley if desired.

Whole grain toasts with Peanut butter

Prep time
5 mins

Cook Time
5 mins

Servings
2 per.

Calorie
180-250 kcal/Toast

Ingredients:

- **4** sslices of whole grain bread

- **4** tablespoons of natural peanut butter (no added sugar or salt)

- **1** banana, sliced (optional for topping)

- **1** tablespoon of chia seeds (optional for topping)

- **1** teaspoon of honey (optional for drizzling)

Instructions:

1.

- Place the 4 slices of whole grain bread in a toaster. Toast until they reach your desired level of crispiness.

- While the bread is toasting, stir the natural peanut butter to ensure it's well-mixed.

- Once the bread is toasted, spread 1 tablespoon of natural peanut butter evenly over each slice.

2.

- Slice the banana and place the slices on top of the peanut butter.

- Sprinkle chia seeds over the banana slices.

- Drizzle a small amount of honey over the toppings for added sweetness, if desired.

Whole-wheat pancakes with fruits

Prep time
10 mins

Cook Time
20 mins

Servings
6 per.

Calorie
150 kcal/Pan.

Ingredients:

- **1 1/2** cups whole-wheat flour
- **2** tablespoons sugar
- **2** teaspoons baking powder
- **1/2** teaspoon baking soda
- **1/2** teaspoon salt
- **1 1/2** cups low-fat buttermilk
- **2** large eggs
- **2** tablespoons vegetable oil or melted coconut oil

- **1** teaspoon vanilla extract
- **1** Cooking spray or a little oil for the pan
- **1** cup mixed fresh berries (strawberries, blueberries, raspberries)
- **1** banana, sliced
- **2** large eggs
- **1/4** cup chopped nuts (optional)
- **1/4** cup pure maple syrup or honey (optional)

Instructions:

1.

- In a large bowl, whisk together the whole-wheat flour, sugar, baking powder, baking soda, and salt.

- In a separate bowl, whisk the buttermilk, eggs, oil, and vanilla extract until well combined.

- Pour the wet ingredients into the dry ingredients and gently mix until just combined. Do not over-mix; a few lumps are fine.

2.

- Heat a non-stick skillet or griddle over medium heat and lightly coat with cooking spray or oil.

- Pour 1/4 cup of batter onto the skillet for each pancake. Cook until bubbles form on the surface, and the edges look set, about 2-3 minutes.

- Flip the pancakes and cook until golden brown on the other side, about 1-2 minutes more.

3.

- Repeat with the remaining batter, adding more cooking spray or oil to the skillet as needed.

- Serve the pancakes warm, topped with fresh mixed berries, banana slices, and a sprinkle of nuts if using.

Whole-grain waffles with fruit

Prep time
10 mins

Cook Time
10 mins

Servings
2 per.

Calorie
350 kcal/Waffle

Ingredients:

- **1** cup whole wheat flour
- **1/2** cup rolled oats
- **2** tablespoons ground flaxseed
- **1** tablespoon baking powder
- **1/4** teaspoon salt
- **1 1/4** cups low-fat milk or almond milk
- **2** large eggs
- **2** tablespoons olive oil or melted coconut oil
- **1** teaspoon vanilla extract

- **1/2** cup fresh blueberries
- **1/2** cup sliced strawberries
- **1/2** cup sliced bananas
- **2** tablespoons pure maple syrup or honey
- **1/4** cup plain Greek yogurt (optional)

Instructions:

- Preheat your waffle iron according to the manufacturer's instructions.

- In a large bowl, combine the whole wheat flour, rolled oats, ground flaxseed, baking powder, and salt.

- In another bowl, whisk together the milk, eggs, olive oil (or melted coconut oil), and vanilla extract.

- Pour the wet ingredients into the dry ingredients and stir until just combined. Be careful not to over-mix.

- Lightly grease the waffle iron with cooking spray or a little oil. Pour the batter onto the preheated waffle iron and cook until golden brown and crisp, about 3-5 minutes, depending on your waffle iron.

- Repeat with the remaining batter.

- While the waffles are cooking, prepare the fruit toppings by washing and slicing the fruits.

- Once the waffles are ready, top them with fresh blueberries, sliced strawberries, and bananas.

- Drizzle with pure maple syrup or honey.

- Add a dollop of plain Greek yogurt on top if desired for extra creaminess and protein.

Whole grain cereal with milk or fruit

Prep time	Cook Time	Servings	Calorie
5 mins	0 mins	2 per.	250-300 kcal

Ingredients::

- **1** cup whole grain cereal (e.g., oats, bran flakes, or multigrain flakes)
- **1** cup skim milk or a plant-based milk alternative (e.g., almond milk, soy milk)
- **1** medium-sized banana, sliced (or any other fruit of your choice: berries, apple slices, etc.)
- **2** tablespoons of nuts (e.g., almonds, walnuts) or seeds (e.g., chia seeds, flaxseeds) for added crunch and nutrition
- **1** teaspoon of honey or maple syrup (optional, for sweetness)

Instructions:

- Divide the whole grain cereal equally into two bowls (1/2 cup each).

- Pour 1/2 cup of skim milk or your chosen milk alternative over the cereal in each bowl.

2.
- Top each bowl with half of the sliced banana or your chosen fruit.
- Sprinkle 1 tablespoon of nuts or seeds over each bowl.
- Drizzle with honey or maple syrup if you prefer a bit of added sweetness.

Egg White Frittata

Prep time
10 mins

Cook Time
15 mins

Servings
2 per.

Calorie
120 kcal/ serving

Ingredients:

- **6** large egg whites
- **1/4** cup skim milk or almond milk
- **1/2** cup spinach, chopped
- **1/4** cup bell peppers, diced (any color)
- **1/4** cup cherry tomatoes, halved
- **1/4** cup onion, finely chopped
- **1/4** cup mushrooms, sliced
- **1/4** cup low-fat feta cheese, crumbled

- **1/2** teaspoon olive oil
- **1/4** teaspoon Salt and pepper to taste
- ***** Fresh herbs for garnish (optional, e.g., parsley or chives)
- **1** clove garlic, minced

Instructions:

1.
- Preheat the Oven: Set your oven to 375°F (190°C).
- Prepare the Vegetables: Chop and dice all the vegetables as listed.
- Whisk Egg Whites: In a medium bowl, whisk together the egg whites, milk, salt, and pepper until well combined.

2.
- Sauté Vegetables: Heat the olive oil in an oven-safe skillet over medium heat. Add the onions and garlic, sautéing for about 2 minutes until they become translucent. Add the bell peppers, mushrooms, and spinach, and cook for another 3-4 minutes until the vegetables are tender.
- Combine Ingredients: Pour the egg white mixture over the sautéed vegetables in the skillet. Sprinkle the cherry tomatoes and feta cheese evenly over the top.

- Cook the Frittata: Allow the frittata to cook on the stovetop for about 2-3 minutes until the edges begin to set.

- Bake: Transfer the skillet to the preheated oven and bake for 10 minutes, or until the egg whites are fully set and the top is lightly golden.

- Garnish and Serve: Remove from the oven and let it cool slightly before slicing. Garnish with fresh herbs if desired.

Scrambled eggs with vegetables

Prep time 10 mins	Cook Time 10 mins	Servings 2 per.	Calorie 200 kcal/ serving

Ingredients: :

- **4** large eggs
- **1/4** cup skim milk or almond milk
- **1** small bell pepper, diced
- **1** small zucchini, diced
- **1/2** cup baby spinach, chopped
- **1** small tomato, diced
- **1/4** cup onion, finely chopped
- **1/4** teaspoon black pepper

- **1/4** teaspoon turmeric (optional)
- **1** tablespoon olive oil or avocado oil
- * Fresh parsley or chives for garnish (optional)

Instructions:

- In a medium bowl, whisk together the eggs, milk, black pepper, and turmeric.

- Heat the olive oil or avocado oil in a non-stick skillet over medium heat.

- Add the diced onion and cook until it becomes translucent, then add the bell pepper and zucchini, cooking for another 3-4 minutes until they start to soften.

- Stir in the chopped tomato and baby spinach, cooking for another 1-2 minutes until the spinach is wilted.

2.

- Pour the egg mixture over the cooked vegetables in the skillet.

- Let it sit for about 30 seconds, then gently stir with a spatula, scraping the bottom of the skillet.

- Continue to cook, stirring occasionally, until the eggs are cooked through but still moist, about 3-4 minutes.

3.

- Divide the scrambled eggs with vegetables onto two plates.

- Garnish with fresh parsley or chives if desired.

Oatmeal with Fruits/Chia

Prep time
5 mins

Cook Time
10 mins

Servings
2 per.

Calorie
280-380 kcal

Ingredients:

- **1** cup rolled oats
- **2** cup water or unsweetened almond milk
- ***** Pinch of salt (optional)
- **1** tsp vanilla extract or honey (optional)

Fruit Variant:

- **1/2** cup mixed berries (blueberries, strawberries, raspberries)
- **1/2** banana, sliced
- **1** tbsp chopped nuts (almonds, walnuts)

Chia Seed Variant:

- **1** tbsp chia seeds
- **1/2** cup diced apples or pears
- **1** tbsp pumpkin seeds
- **1** cinnamon

Instructions:

- In a medium-sized pot, bring water or almond milk to a boil.

- Add rolled oats and a pinch of salt if using. Reduce heat to a simmer.

- Cook, stirring occasionally, for about 5-7 minutes, or until the oats have absorbed the liquid and reached your desired consistency.

- Stir in vanilla extract or honey if desired.

Fruit Variant:

2.
- Once the base oatmeal is ready, divide it into two bowls.

- Top each bowl with 1/4 cup mixed berries, 1/4 banana slices, and 1/2 tbsp chopped nuts if desired and serve.

Chia Seed Variant:

2.
- While the base oatmeal is cooking, soak the chia seeds in a small bowl with 2 tablespoons of water. Let sit for about 5 minutes until they form a gel-like consistency.

- Once the base oatmeal is ready, divide it into two bowls.

- Stir the soaked chia seeds into each bowl.

- Top each bowl with 1/4 cup diced apples or pears, 1/2 tbsp pumpkin seeds, and a sprinkle of cinnamon and serve.

Overnight oats with fruit

Prep time	Cook Time	Servings	Calorie
10 mins	Overnight	2 per.	300 kcal/serving

Ingredients:

- **1** cup rolled oats
- **1** cup unsweetened almond milk
- **1** tbsp chia seeds
- **1** tbsp honey or maple syrup (optional)
- **1/2** tsp vanilla extract
- **1/2** tsp ground cinnamon

- **1/2** cup fresh berries (strawberries, blueberries, raspberries, or a mix)
- **1** medium banana, sliced
- **1** tbsp chopped nuts (almonds, walnuts, or pecans)
- **1** tbsp unsweetened shredded coconut (optional)

Instructions:

1.
- In a medium-sized bowl, combine the rolled oats, almond milk, chia seeds, honey or maple syrup (if using), vanilla extract, and ground cinnamon. Stir well to ensure all ingredients are evenly mixed.

2.
- Divide the mixture into two mason jars or bowls with lids.
- Top each jar or bowl with half of the fresh berries, banana slices, chopped nuts, and shredded coconut (if using).

3.
- Cover the jars or bowls with lids and refrigerate overnight, or for at least 4 hours, to allow the oats and chia seeds to absorb the liquid and soften.
- In the morning, give the oats a good stir and add a splash of almond milk if you prefer a thinner consistency. Serve & enjoy.

Yogurt parfait with mixed berries

Prep time
10 mins

Cook Time
0 mins

Servings
2 per.

Calorie
200 kcal/serving

Ingredients:

- **1** cup low-fat Greek yogurt
- **1/2** cup fresh strawberries, hulled & sliced
- **1/2** cup fresh blueberries
- **1/2** cup fresh raspberries
- **1/4** cup granola (preferably low-sugar, whole grain)

- **2** tsp honey (optional)
- **1** tbsp chia seeds (optional)
- ***** Fresh mint leaves for garnish (optional)

Instructions:

1.
- Wash and prepare the strawberries, blueberries, and raspberries.
- Slice the strawberries if they are not already sliced.

2.
- Take two serving glasses or bowls.
- Start by adding 1/4 cup of Greek yogurt to the bottom of each glass.
- Add a layer of strawberries on top of the yogurt.
- Add another 1/4 cup of Greek yogurt on top of the strawberries.

2.
- Add a layer of blueberries and raspberries.
- Add the remaining Greek yogurt on top of the berries.

3.
- Sprinkle the granola evenly over the top of the yogurt layers in each glass.
- Drizzle 1 teaspoon of honey over each parfait, if using.
- Sprinkle 1/2 tablespoon of chia seeds over each parfait, if using & garnish.

Smoothie with berries and chia

Prep time	Cook Time	Servings	Calorie
5 mins	5 mins	2 per.	160 kcal

Ingredients:

- **1** cup mixed berries (fresh or frozen)
- **1** banana
- **1** cup unsweetened almond milk (or any plant-based milk of choice)
- **2** tbsp chia seeds
- **1** tbsp honey or maple syrup (optional)
- **1/2** cup Greek yogurt (optional for extra creaminess and protein)
- * A handful of spinach (optional for extra nutrients)
- **1/2** tsp vanilla extract (optional)
- *Ice cubes (optional, for a colder smoothie)

Instructions:

1.
- Wash the berries if using fresh ones.
- Peel the banana.
- If using spinach, wash and dry it.

2.
- In a blender, add the mixed berries, banana, almond milk, chia seeds, honey or maple syrup (if using), Greek yogurt (if using), spinach (if using), and vanilla extract (if using).
- Blend until smooth. If you prefer a thicker smoothie, add ice cubes and blend again until the desired consistency is reached.
- Pour the smoothie into two glasses.

Smoothie with mango and spinach

Prep time
5 mins

Cook Time
0 mins

Servings
2 per.

Calorie
200 kcal

Ingredients:

- **1** cup fresh spinach leaves
- **1** cup frozen mango chunks
- **1** banana
- **1** cup unsweetened almond milk

- **1** tbsp chia seeds
- **1** tbsp honey (optional)
- **1** tsp fresh lemon juice

Instructions:

1.

- Rinse the fresh spinach leaves thoroughly.
- Peel and slice the banana.
- Add the fresh spinach leaves, frozen mango chunks, banana, and unsweetened almond milk to a blender.
- Blend until smooth and creamy.
- Add the chia seeds and blend for another 10-15 sec. to incorporate them evenly.

2.

- If you prefer a sweeter smoothie, add 1 Tbsp of honey and blend again for a few seconds.
- Add 1 tsp of fresh lemon juice to enhance the flavor.
- Give the smoothie one final blend to mix everything together.
- Pour the smoothie into two glasses & serve.

Smoothie with blueberries

Prep time
5 mins

Cook Time
0 mins

Servings
2 per.

Calorie
150-200 kcal

Ingredients:

- **1** cup fresh or frozen blueberries
- **1** medium banana
- **1** cup spinach (optional for added nutrients)
- **1** cup unsweetened almond milk (or any other plant-based milk)
- **1** tbsp chia seeds
- **1** tbsp honey or maple syrup (optional)
- **1/2** tsp vanilla extract
- **1/2** cup plain Greek yogurt (optional for added protein)
- * Ice cubes (optional for desired thickness)

Instructions::

1.
- If using fresh blueberries, rinse them thoroughly.
- Peel the banana and break it into chunks.
- Measure out the spinach, almond milk, chia seeds, honey/maple syrup, vanilla extract, and Greek yogurt (if using).

2.
- Add the blueberries, banana, spinach (if using), almond milk, chia seeds, honey/maple syrup, vanilla extract, and Greek yogurt (if using) into a blender.
- Blend on high until smooth and creamy. If you prefer a thicker smoothie, add a few ice cubes and blend again.
- Pour the smoothie into two glasses & serve.

Smoothie bowl with berries & seeds

Prep time
10 mins

Cook Time
0 mins

Servings
2 per.

Calorie
300 kcal

Smoothie Base:

- **1** cup frozen mixed berries (strawberries, blueberries, raspberries)
- **1** medium banana
- **1** cup unsweetened almond milk
- **1** tbsp chia seeds
- **1** tbsp ground flaxseed
- **1** tbsp honey (optional)

Toppings:

- **1/4** cup fresh blueberries
- **1/4** cup sliced strawberries
- **2** tbsp granola (preferably low-sugar)
- **1** tbsp pumpkin seeds
- **1** tbsp sunflower seeds
- **1** tbsp unsweetened shredded coconut
- **1** tsp chia seeds
- **1** tsp ground flaxseed

Instructions:

1.
- In a blender, combine the frozen mixed berries, banana, almond milk, chia seeds, ground flaxseed, and honey (if using).
- Blend until smooth and thick. If the mixture is too thick, add a little more almond milk until the desired consistency is achieved.

2.
- Pour the smoothie base into two bowls.
- Evenly distribute the fresh blueberries, sliced strawberries, granola, pumpkin seeds, sunflower seeds, shredded coconut, chia seeds, and ground flaxseed on top of the smoothie base.
- Serve & enjoy.

Greek yogurt with honey and nuts / granola

Prep time
5 mins

Cook Time
0 mins

Servings
2 per.

Calorie
220-250 kcal

For the base:

- **2** cups of plain Greek yogurt (low-fat or fat-free)

For the honey and nuts variant:

- **2** tbsp of honey
- **1/4** cup of mixed nuts (almonds, walnuts, pistachios), roughly chopped

For the granola variant:

- **1/4** cup of heart-healthy granola (low-sugar, high-fiber)

Instructions:

1.
- Divide the Greek yogurt evenly into two bowls.

Honey and Nuts Variant:

2.
- Drizzle 1 tablespoon of honey over each bowl of yogurt.
- Sprinkle 1/8 cup of mixed nuts over the top of each bowl.

Granola Variant:

2.
- Sprinkle 1/8 cup of granola over the top of each bowl of yogurt.

Cottage cheese with fruits

Prep time
10 mins

Cook Time
0 mins

Servings
2 per.

Calorie
150-160 kcal

Base Ingredients:

- **1** cup low-fat cottage cheese
- **1** tbsp honey or maple syrup (optional, for sweetness)
- * Fresh mint leaves for garnish (optional)

Pineapple Variant:

- **1/2** cup fresh pineapple chunks
- **1/4** cup sliced strawberries
- **1** tbsp unsweetened coconut flakes

Blueberry Variant:

- **1/2** cup fresh blueberries
- **1** tbsp chopped walnuts or almonds

Raspberry Variant:

- **1/2** cup fresh raspberries
- **1** tbsp chopped fresh mint (optional)

Strawberry Variant:

- **1/2** cup fresh strawberries, sliced
- **1** tbsp chopped fresh basil (optional)

Preparation for All Variants:

1.
- Divide the cottage cheese equally into two bowls (1/2 cup per bowl).
- If using, drizzle each bowl with half of the honey or maple syrup (1/2 tablespoon per bowl).

Pineapple Variant:

2.
- Top one bowl of cottage cheese with the pineapple chunks.
- Sprinkle with unsweetened coconut flakes.
- Garnish with a few mint leaves, if desired.

Blueberry Variant:

2.
- Top the other bowl of cottage cheese with the fresh blueberries.
- Sprinkle with chopped walnuts or almonds.
- Garnish with a few mint leaves, if desired.

Raspberry Variant:

2.
- Divide the cottage cheese mixture evenly between two bowls.
- Top each bowl with 1/4 cup of fresh raspberries.
- Garnish with chopped fresh mint if desired.

Strawberry Variant:

2.
- Divide the cottage cheese mixture evenly between two bowls.
- Top each bowl with 1/4 cup of sliced fresh strawberries.
- Garnish with chopped fresh basil if desired.

Quinoa fruit salat

Prep time	Cook Time	Servings	Calorie
15 mins	15 mins	2 per.	280 kcal/serving

Ingredients:

- **1/2** cup quinoa, rinsed
- **1** cup water
- **1/2** cup strawberries, hulled and quartered
- **1/2** cup mango, diced
- **1** kiwi, peeled and sliced
- **1/2** cup pomegranate seeds

Dressing:

- **1** tbsp honey
- **1** tbsp fresh lime juice
- **1** tsp lime zest
- **1** tbsp fresh mint, finely chopped

Instructions:

1.
- In a medium saucepan, bring 1 cup of water to a boil.
- Add the rinsed quinoa, reduce the heat to low, cover, and simmer for about 15 minutes, or until the quinoa is tender and the water is absorbed.
- Remove from heat and let it sit, covered, for 5 minutes. Fluff with a fork and let it cool completely.

2.

- While the quinoa is cooling, prepare the fruit. Hull and quarter the strawberries, dice the mango, slice the kiwi, and gather the blueberries and pomegranate seeds.

- In a small bowl, whisk together the honey, fresh lime juice, lime zest, and chopped mint.

3.

- In a large bowl, combine the cooled quinoa and prepared fruit.

- Pour the dressing over the quinoa and fruit mixture. Gently toss to coat all the ingredients evenly.

- Divide the salad into two serving bowls & serve.

04

Chapter

Lunch

Spinach and Chicken Salad

Prep time
15 mins

Cook Time
20 mins

Servings
2 per.

Calorie
350 kcal

For the Salad:

- **2** cups fresh spinach leaves
- **1** cup cooked chicken breast, sliced
- **1/2** cup cherry tomatoes, halved
- **1/4** cup red onion, thinly sliced
- **1/4** cup cucumber, diced
- **1/4** cup avocado, diced
- **2** tbsp sunflower seeds

For the Dressing:

- **2** tbsp olive oil
- **1** tbsp balsamic vinegar
- **1** tsp Dijon mustard
- **1** tsp honey
- **1** clove garlic, minced
- *****Salt and pepper to taste

Instructions:

1.

- In a large bowl, combine the spinach leaves, sliced chicken breast, cherry tomatoes, red onion, cucumber, and avocado.

- Toss the ingredients gently to mix them well.

2.

- In a small bowl, whisk together the olive oil, balsamic vinegar, Dijon mustard, honey, minced garlic, salt, and pepper until well combined.

- Pour the dressing over the salad mixture and toss gently to coat all the ingredients evenly.

3.

- Sprinkle sunflower seeds on top for added crunch & serve.

Grilled Chicken Caesar Salad

Prep time
15 mins

Cook Time
15 mins

Servings
2 per.

Calorie
350 kcal

For the Salad:

- **2** boneless, skinless chicken breasts
- **4** cups romaine lettuce, chopped
- **1/2** cup cherry tomatoes, halved
- **1/4** cup grated Parmesan cheese
- **1/4** cup whole grain croutons (optional)
- **1** tbsp olive oil (for grilling the chicken)

For the Dressing:

- **1/4** cup Greek yogurt (non-fat)
- **1** tbsp extra virgin olive oil
- **1** tbsp lemon juice
- **1** tsp Dijon mustard
- **1** clove garlic, minced
- **1** tsp Worcestershire sauce
- **1** tbsp grated Parmesan cheese
- ***** Salt and pepper to taste

Instructions:

1.
- Preheat the grill to medium-high heat.
- Brush the chicken breasts with olive oil and season with salt and pepper.
- Grill the chicken for about 6-7 minutes on each side, or until the internal temp. reaches 165°F (74°C).
- Remove from the grill and let rest for a few minutes, then slice into thin strips.

2.
- In a small bowl, combine Greek yogurt, extra virgin olive oil, lemon juice, Dijon mustard, minced garlic, Worcestershire sauce, and grated Parmesan cheese.
- Mix well until smooth and creamy.
- Season with salt and pepper to taste.

3.
- In a large bowl, combine the chopped romaine lettuce, cherry tomatoes, and grated Parmesan cheese.
- Add the grilled chicken strips on top.

- Drizzle the Caesar dressing over the salad and toss gently to coat all ingredients evenly.

- Sprinkle with whole grain croutons if desired.

- Divide the salad into two servings & serve.

Caprese Salad

Prep time
10 mins

Cook Time
15 mins

Servings
2 per.

Calorie
250 kcal

Ingredients:

- **2** large ripe tomatoes, sliced
- **8** oz (225g) fresh mozzarella cheese, sliced
- **1** cup fresh basil leaves
- **2** tbsp extra virgin olive oil
- **1** tbsp balsamic vinegar
- * Salt and ground black pepper to taste

Instructions:

1.
- Slice the tomatoes and mozzarella cheese into approximately 1/4 inch thick slices.
- Arrange the tomato and mozzarella slices on a large platter or individual plates.
- Tuck fresh basil leaves between the slices.

2.
- Drizzle the extra virgin olive oil and balsamic vinegar over the salad.
- Season with salt and freshly ground black pepper to taste.

Quinoa salad with chickpeas/veggies

Prep time
15 mins

Cook Time
20 mins

Servings
2 per.

Calorie
400 kcal

Ingredients:

- **1/2** cup quinoa (uncooked)
- **1** cup water
- **2** tbsp olive oil
- **1** tbsp lemon juice
- **1** tsp lemon zest
- **1/2** tsp ground cumin
- **1/2** tsp paprika
- * Salt and pepper to taste
- **2** tbsp fresh parsley, chopped
- **1** tbsp fresh mint, chopped

Chickpeas Variant:

- **1** can (15 oz) chickpeas, drained and rinsed

Veggie Variant:

- **1/2** cup cherry tomatoes, halved
- **1/2** cup cucumber, diced
- **1/4** cup red bell pepper, diced
- **1/4** cup red onion, finely chopped

Instructions:

1.

- Rinse the quinoa under cold water.
- In a medium saucepan, bring 1 cup of water to a boil.
- Add the quinoa, reduce heat to low, cover, and simmer for about 15 minutes or until the water is absorbed and the quinoa is tender.
- Fluff with a fork and let it cool.

For the Chickpeas Variant:

2.

- In a large bowl, combine the cooked quinoa and chickpeas.
- Add 1 tbsp olive oil, lemon juice, lemon zest, cumin, paprika, salt, and pepper.
- Mix well to combine.

For the Veggie Variant:

2.
- In a large bowl, combine the cooked quinoa, cherry tomatoes, cucumber, red bell pepper, and red onion.
- Add 1 tbsp olive oil, lemon juice, lemon zest, cumin, paprika, salt, and pepper.
- Mix well to combine.

3.
- For both versions, add fresh parsley and mint to the bowl.
- Toss gently to mix the herbs throughout the salad.
- Divide the salad into two portions & serve.

Quinoa and black bean salad

Prep time	Cook Time	Servings	Calorie
15 mins	15 mins	2 per.	350 kcal

Ingredients:

- **1/2** cup quinoa
- **1** cup water
- **1** can (15 oz) black beans, rinsed and drained
- **1/2** red bell pepper, chopped
- **1/2** yellow bell pepper, chopped
- **1/2** cup cherry tomatoes, halved
- **1/4** cup red onion, finely chopped

- **1/4** cup fresh cilantro, chopped
- **1/4** cup feta cheese, crumbled (optional)
- **2** tbsp olive oil
- **2** tbsp lime juice
- **1** tsp cumin
- **1/2** tsp garlic powder
- ***** Salt and pepper to taste

Instructions:

- Rinse the quinoa under cold water.
- In a medium saucepan, combine quinoa and water.
- Bring to a boil, then reduce heat to low, cover, and simmer for 15 minutes or until quinoa is tender and water is absorbed.
- Remove from heat and let it sit for 5 minutes, then fluff with a fork.

2.
- In a small bowl, whisk together olive oil, lime juice, cumin, garlic powder, salt, and pepper.

3.
- In a large bowl, combine cooked quinoa, black beans, red bell pepper, yellow bell pepper, cherry tomatoes, red onion, and cilantro.
- Pour the dressing over the salad and toss to combine.
- Top with feta cheese if desired.
- Chill in the refrigerator for at least 30 minutes (optional) & serve.

Tomato and mozzarella salad

Prep time	Cook Time	Servings	Calorie
10 mins	0 mins	2 per.	250 kcal

Ingredients:

- **2** large tomatoes, sliced
- **4** oz (113 g) fresh mozzarella cheese, sliced
- **1/4** cup fresh basil leaves
- **2** tbsp extra virgin olive oil
- **1** tbsp balsamic vinegar
- **1/4** tsp sea salt
- **1/4** tsp freshly ground black pepper

Instructions:

1.
- Wash and slice the tomatoes into thin, even slices.
- Slice the mozzarella cheese into similar-sized pieces.
- Wash and pat dry the basil leaves.

2.
- On a large plate, arrange the tomato and mozzarella slices in an alternating pattern (tomato slice, mozzarella slice, basil leaf).
- Continue until all slices are arranged on the plate.

3.

- Drizzle the extra virgin olive oil evenly over the tomatoes and mozzarella.

- Follow with the balsamic vinegar.

- Sprinkle the sea salt and freshly ground black pepper over the top.

- Tear a few additional basil leaves and sprinkle them over the top for garnish & serve.

Garbanzo Bean Salad with Pitas

Prep time
15 mins

Cook Time
0 mins

Servings
2 per.

Calorie
300 kcal

Ingredients:

- **1** cup canned garbanzo beans (chickpeas), drained and rinsed
- **1/2** cup diced cucumber
- **1/2** cup diced tomatoes
- **1/4** cup diced red onion
- **1/4** cup chopped fresh parsley
- **2** tbsp crumbled feta cheese (optional)

- **1** tbsp olive oil
- **1** tbsp lemon juice
- *Salt and pepper to taste
- **2** whole wheat pitas

Instructions:

1.

- In a bowl, combine the garbanzo beans, cucumber, tomatoes, red onion, & parsley.

- Add the olive oil and lemon juice to the bowl. Season with salt and pepper to taste.

- Gently toss all ingredients until well mixed.

2.

- Divide the salad into two equal portions.

- Serve each portion with a whole wheat pita.

Chickpea salad with veggies / avocado

Prep time
15 mins

Cook Time
0 mins

Servings
2 per.

Calorie
350 kcal

Ingredients:

- **1** can (15 oz) chickpeas, drained and rinsed
- **1** cup cherry tomatoes, halved
- **1/2** cucumber, diced
- **1/4** red onion, finely chopped
- **2** tbsp fresh parsley, chopped
- **2** tbsp fresh lemon juice
- **1** tbsp extra virgin olive oil
- * Salt and pepper to taste

Veggie Variant:

- **1/2** bell pepper (any color), diced
- **1/4** cup shredded carrots

Avocado Variant:

- **1** ripe avocado, diced

Base Preparation:

1.

- Drain and rinse the chickpeas, then place them in a large mixing bowl.
- Halve the cherry tomatoes, dice the cucumber, and finely chop the red onion.
- Add the cherry tomatoes, cucumber, red onion, and parsley to the bowl with the chickpeas.
- In a small bowl, whisk together the lemon juice, olive oil, salt, and pepper. Pour the dressing over the salad and toss to combine.

Veggie Variant:

2.

- Dice the bell pepper and shred the carrots.
- Add the bell pepper and shredded carrots to the base salad mixture. Toss to combine & serve.

Avocado Variant:

2.

- Dice the avocado just before serving to prevent browning.
- Gently fold the diced avocado into the base salad mixture & serve.

Turkey salad with mixed greens

Prep time
10 mins

Cook Time
0 mins

Servings
2 per.

Calorie
300 kcal

Ingredients:

- **2** cups mixed greens (spinach, arugula, kale)
- **1** cup cooked turkey breast, shredded or diced
- **1/2** cup cherry tomatoes, halved
- **1/2** cup cucumber, sliced
- **1/4** cup red bell pepper, diced
- **1/4** Cup red onion, thinly sliced
- **1/4** cup avocado, diced

- **2** tbsp olive oil
- **1** tbsp balsamic vinegar
- **1** tsp Dijon mustard
- ***** Salt and pepper to taste
- **1** tbsp sunflower seeds (optional)

Prepare the Ingredients:

- Wash and dry the mixed greens.
- Shred or dice the cooked turkey breast.
- Halve the cherry tomatoes, slice the cucumber, dice the red bell pepper, thinly slice the red onion, and dice the avocado.

Make the Dressing:

- In a small bowl, whisk together the olive oil, balsamic vinegar, Dijon mustard, salt, and pepper until well combined.

Assemble the Salad:

- In a large bowl, combine the mixed greens, turkey, cherry tomatoes, cucumber, red bell pepper, red onion, and avocado.
- Drizzle the dressing over the salad and toss gently to combine.
- Sprinkle sunflower seeds on top for added crunch and nutrition & serve.

Tuna & avocado salad

Prep time
15 mins

Cook Time
0 mins

Servings
2 per.

Calorie
350 kcal

Ingredients:

- **1** can (5 oz) tuna in water, drained
- **1** ripe avocado, diced
- **1** cup mixed greens (spinach, arugula, or your choice)
- **1/2** cup cherry tomatoes, halved
- **1/4** cup red onion, finely sliced

- **1** tbsp olive oil
- **1** tbsp lemon juice
- **1** tsp Dijon mustard
- ***** Salt and pepper to taste
- **1** tbsp chopped fresh herbs (parsley, cilantro, or dill) optional

Instructions:

1.
- Drain the canned tuna and place it in a large mixing bowl.
- Dice the avocado and add it to the bowl with the tuna.
- Halve the cherry tomatoes and finely slice the red onion; add them to the bowl.
- Add the mixed greens to the bowl with the other ingredients.

2.
- In a small bowl, whisk together the olive oil, lemon juice, Dijon mustard, salt, and pepper until well combined.

3.
- Pour the dressing over the tuna and vegetable mixture.
- Gently toss everything together until well coated.
- Optionally, sprinkle with chopped fresh herbs.

Tuna salad with mixed greens

Prep time	Cook Time	Servings	Calorie
15 mins	35 mins	2 per.	250 kcal

For the Salad:

- **1** can (5 oz) tuna in water, drained
- **4** cups mixed salad greens (e.g., spinach, arugula, romaine)
- **1/2** cup cherry tomatoes, halved
- **1/4** cup cucumber, sliced
- **1/4** cup red onion, thinly sliced
- **1/4** cup shredded carrots
- **1/4** avocado, diced

For the Dressing:

- **2** tbsp olive oil
- **1** tbsp lemon juice
- **1** tsp Dijon mustard
- **1** tsp honey
- *****Salt and pepper to taste

Instructions:

1.
- In a large bowl, combine the mixed salad greens, cherry tomatoes, cucumber, red onion, and shredded carrots.
- Gently mix in the drained tuna and diced avocado.

2.
- In a small bowl, whisk together the olive oil, lemon juice, Dijon mustard, honey, salt, and pepper until well combined.

3.
- Drizzle the dressing over the salad and toss gently to coat all the ingredients evenly.
- Serve.

Lentil soup

Prep time
10 mins

Cook Time
35 mins

Servings
2 per.

Calorie
300 kcal

Ingredients:

- **1** cup lentils, rinsed
- **1** tbsp olive oil
- **1** medium onion, diced
- **2** cloves garlic, minced
- **1** carrot, diced
- **1** celery stalk, diced
- **1** tsp ground cumin
- **1** tsp ground coriander
- **1/2** tsp turmeric
- **1/2** tsp smoked paprika

- **1/4** tsp black pepper
- **1/4** tsp salt (optional)
- **4** cups low-sodium vegetable broth
- **1** can (14.5 oz) diced tomatoes, with juice
- **1** bay leaf
- **1/2** tsp dried thyme
- **1/2** tsp dried rosemary
- **1** tbsp lemon juice
- *Fresh parsley, chopped (for garnish)

Instructions:

1.
- In a large pot, heat olive oil over medium heat.
- Add diced onion, garlic, carrot, and celery. Sauté until vegetables are softened, about 5 minutes.

2.
- Stir in cumin, coriander, turmeric, smoked paprika, black pepper, and salt. Cook for 1 minute until fragrant.
- Add lentils, vegetable broth, diced tomatoes (with juice), bay leaf, thyme, and rosemary. Stir to combine.

3.
- Bring the soup to a boil, then reduce heat to low and simmer for 25-30 minutes, or until lentils are tender.
- Remove and discard the bay leaf.
- Stir in lemon juice. Adjust seasoning to taste.
- Garnish with fresh parsley before serving.

Veggie/Chicken soup

Prep time
15 mins

Cook Time
30 mins

Servings
2 per.

Calorie
200/300 kcal

Ingredients:

- **1** tbsp olive oil
- **1** small onion, diced
- **2** cloves garlic, minced
- **2** medium carrots, sliced
- **2** celery stalks, sliced
- **1** tsp dried thyme
- **1** tsp dried rosemary
- **4** cups low-sodium chicken or vegetable broth
- **1** bay leaf
- ***Salt and pepper to taste

Vegetable Variant:

- **1** cup diced potatoes
- **1** cup chopped kale or spinach
- **1** can (15 oz) diced tomatoes, undrained

Veggie Variant:

- **1** chicken breast, diced (about 6 oz)
- **1** cup diced potatoes
- **1** cup chopped kale or spinach

Instructions:

- Dice the onion, slice the carrots and celery, mince the garlic, and dice the potatoes. If using the chicken variant, dice the chicken breast into bite-sized pieces.
- In a large pot, heat the olive oil over medium heat.
- Add the diced onion and cook until softened, about 3-4 minutes.
- Add the minced garlic, sliced carrots, and celery. Cook for another 5 minutes until the vegetables begin to soften.

- Stir in the dried thyme and rosemary. Cook for 1 minute to release the flavors.
- Pour in the low-sodium broth and add the bay leaf. Bring to a simmer.

Vegetable Variant:

- Add the diced potatoes and can of diced tomatoes (with liquid) to the pot.

- Simmer for 20 minutes until the potatoes are tender.

- Add the chopped kale or spinach. Cook for another 5 minutes until the greens are wilted.

- Season with salt and pepper to taste. Remove the bay leaf before serving.

Chicken Variant:

- Add the diced potatoes and chicken to the pot.

- Simmer for 20 minutes until the potatoes are tender and the chicken is cooked.

- Add the chopped kale or spinach. Cook for another 5 minutes.

- Season with salt and pepper to taste. Remove the bay leaf before serving.

Chicken/Turkey wrap with veggies

Prep time
15 mins

Cook Time
10 mins

Servings
2 per.

Calorie
350 kcal

Ingredients:

- **2** whole wheat tortillas
- **1/2** cup shredded carrots
- **1/2** cup thinly sliced bell peppers (red, yellow, or green)
- **1/2** cup chopped cucumbers
- **1/4** cup thinly sliced red onion
- **1/2** avocado, sliced
- **1** cup mixed greens (spinach, arugula, or lettuce)
- **2** tbsp hummus

- **2** tbsp low-fat Greek yogurt
- **1** tsp olive oil
- ***** Salt and pepper to taste
- **1/2** tsp garlic powder
- **1/2** tsp paprika

Chicken Variant:

- **1** boneless, skinless chicken breast (about 6 oz)

Turkey Variant:

- **1** boneless, skinless turkey breast (about 6 oz)

Meat preperation:

1.

- Season the Meat: Rub the chicken or turkey breast with olive oil, garlic powder, paprika, salt, and pepper.

- Preheat a grill or skillet over medium-high heat.

- Cook the chicken or turkey breast for about 5 minutes on each side or until the internal temperature reaches 165°F (74°C).

- Remove from heat and let it rest for a few minutes before slicing thinly.Season with salt and pepper to taste. Remove the bay leaf before serving.

Wrap preperation:

2.

- Place the whole wheat tortillas flat on a clean surface.

- Evenly spread 1 tablespoon of hummus on each tortilla.

- Layer the shredded carrots, bell peppers, cucumbers, red onion, avocado slices, and mixed greens on top of the hummus.

- Place the sliced chicken or turkey on top of the vegetables.

- Drizzle 1 tablespoon of low-fat Greek yogurt over the fillings in each wrap.

- Wrap It Up: Fold the sides of the tortilla over the fillings, then roll tightly from the bottom up.

- Cut the wraps in half diagonally and serve immediately.

Veggie Burger on Whole Grain Bun

Prep time 15 mins	Cook Time 20 mins	Servings 2 per.	Calorie 350 kcal

For the Veggie Patty:

- **1** cup black beans, drained and rinsed
- **1/2** cup cooked quinoa
- **1/2** cup grated carrots
- **1/4** cup finely chopped onion

- **2** cloves garlic, minced
- **1/4** cup whole wheat breadcrumbs
- **1** tbsp flaxseed meal mixed with 3 tbsp water (flax egg)

- **1** tsp cumin
- **1** tsp smoked paprika
- **1/2** tsp salt
- **1/4** tsp black pepper
- **2** tbsp olive oil (for cooking)

* For Assembling the Burger:

- **2** whole grain buns
- **4** leaves of lettuce
- **2** slices of tomato
- **1/4** cup sliced red onion
- **2** tbsp hummus or avocado spread (optional)

Preparing the Veggie Patties:

1.
- In a large mixing bowl, mash the black beans with a fork until mostly smooth.
- Add the cooked quinoa, grated carrots, chopped onion, minced garlic, whole wheat breadcrumbs, and the flax egg (flaxseed meal mixed with water). Stir to combine.
- Season with cumin, smoked paprika, salt, and black pepper. Mix well until all ingredients are evenly distributed.
- Form the mixture into 2 patties.

2.
- Heat olive oil in a large skillet over medium heat.
- Add the patties to the skillet and cook for about 4-5 minutes on each side, until they are golden brown and heated through.

3.
- Toast the whole grain buns if desired.
- Spread a thin layer of hummus or avocado spread on the bottom half of each bun
- Place a lettuce leaf on the bottom bun, followed by a veggie patty, a slice of tomato, and some red onion slices.
- Top with the other half of the bun & serve.

Taco chicken bowl

Prep time
15 mins

Cook Time
0 mins

Servings
2 per.

Calorie
300 kcal

Ingredients:

- **2** boneless, skinless chicken breasts (about 6 oz each)
- **1** tsp olive oil
- **1** tsp chili powder
- **1/2** tsp cumin
- **1/2** tsp garlic powder
- **1/2** tsp onion powder
- **1/4** tsp paprika
- **1/4** tsp black pepper
- **1/4** tsp salt
- **1/2** cup quinoa, uncooked

- **1** cup low-sodium chicken broth
- **1** cup black beans, drained and rinsed
- **1** cup corn kernels (fresh, canned, or frozen)
- **1** red bell pepper, diced
- **1** small avocado, diced
- **1** lime, cut into wedges
- * Fresh cilantro, chopped (optional)
- * Salsa or pico de gallo (optional)

Prepare the Quinoa:

- Rinse the quinoa under cold water.

- In a medium saucepan, combine quinoa and chicken broth. Bring to a boil, then reduce to a simmer, cover, and cook for about 15 minutes or until the liquid is absorbed. Fluff with a fork and set aside.

Prepare the Chicken:

- Preheat your grill or a grill pan to medium-high heat.

- Mix together in a bowl the chili powder, cumin, garlic powder, onion powder, paprika, black pepper, and salt.

- Rub the olive oil over the chicken breasts, then coat evenly with the spice mixture.

2.
- Grill the chicken for about 5-7 minutes on each side or until the internal temperature reaches 165°F (75°C).
- Remove the chicken from the grill and let it rest for 5 minutes before slicing.

Assemble the Bowls:

3.
- Divide the cooked quinoa between two bowls.
- Top each bowl with black beans, corn, and diced bell pepper.
- Slice the grilled chicken and add it to the bowls.
- Add diced avocado on top.
- Garnish with lime wedges and fresh cilantro if desired.
- Serve with salsa or pico de gallo on the side.

Turkey and avocado sandwich

Prep time
10 mins

Cook Time
05 mins

Servings
2 per.

Calorie
350 kcal

Ingredients:

- **4** slices whole grain bread
- **6** oz. (about 170g) turkey breast, thinly sliced
- **1** ripe avocado
- **1** small tomato, sliced
- **1/4** cup (60g) baby spinach leaves

- **2** tbsp. (30g) low-fat Greek yogurt
- **1** tbsp. (15ml) lemon juice
- **1** tsp. (5ml) olive oil
- ***** Salt and pepper to taste

Instructions:

1.
- In a small bowl, mash the ripe avocado.
- Add 1 tbsp. lemon juice, 2 tbsp. low-fat Greek yogurt, and a pinch of salt and pepper.
- Mix until smooth and well combined.

2.

- Lightly toast the whole grain bread slices.

- Spread the avocado mixture evenly on one side of each bread slice.

- Layer half of the baby spinach leaves on two of the bread slices.

- Place 3 oz. of turkey breast slices on top of the spinach.

- Add tomato slices on top of the turkey.

- Top with the remaining spinach leaves.

- Cover with the other bread slices, avocado side down & serve.

Turkey and quinoa bowl

Prep time
15 mins

Cook Time
25 mins

Servings
2 per.

Calorie
450 kcal

For the Turkey Marinade:

- **1** lb ground turkey
- **1** tbsp olive oil
- **1** tsp garlic powder
- **1** tsp onion powder
- **1** tsp smoked paprika
- **1/2** tsp black pepper
- **1/2** tsp salt

For the Quinoa:

- **1** cup quinoa
- **2** cups low-sodium chicken broth or water

For the Veggies:

- **1** cup cherry tomatoes, halved
- **1** cup cucumber, diced
- **1/2** cup red bell pepper, diced
- **1/4** cup red onion, finely chopped
- **1** avocado, sliced
- **2** cups baby spinach

For the Dressing:

- **2** tbsp lemon juice
- **1** tbsp olive oil
- **1** tsp honey
- **1/2** tsp Dijon mustard
- *Salt and pepper to taste

Marinate the Turkey:

- In a bowl, mix the ground turkey with olive oil, garlic powder, onion powder, smoked paprika, black pepper, and salt.
- Cover and refrigerate for at least 30 minutes to allow flavors to meld.

Cook the Quinoa:

- Rinse the quinoa under cold water.
- In a medium saucepan, combine quinoa and low-sodium chicken broth (or water).
- Bring to a boil, then reduce to a simmer, cover, and cook for about 15 minutes or until all the liquid is absorbed.
- Fluff with a fork and set aside.

Cook the Turkey:

- In a large skillet, heat 1 tbsp of olive oil over medium-high heat.
- *Add the marinated turkey and cook, breaking it apart with a spoon, until browned and fully cooked, about 7-10 minutes.

Prepare the Dressing:

- In a small bowl, whisk together lemon juice, olive oil, honey, Dijon mustard, salt, and pepper.

Assemble the Bowl:

- In two serving bowls, divide the cooked quinoa as the base.
- Top with cooked turkey, cherry tomatoes, cucumber, red bell pepper, red onion, avocado slices, and baby spinach.
- Drizzle with the prepared dressing & serve.

05

—— **Chapter** ——

Dinner

Baked salmon with veggies/brown rice

Prep time
20 mins

Cook Time
30 mins

Servings
2 per.

Calorie
400-500 kcal

Baked Salmon:

- **2** salmon fillets (about 6 oz each)
- **1** tbsp olive oil
- **1** lemon (half for juice, half sliced)
- **1** tsp garlic powder
- **1** tsp dried dill
- *Salt and pepper to taste

Brown Rice Variant:

- **1** cup brown rice
- **2** cups water

Steamed Veggies Variant:

- **1** cup broccoli florets
- **1** cup baby carrots
- **1** cup snap peas
- **1** tbsp olive oil
- **1** tsp lemon zest
- * Salt and pepper to taste

- **1** tbsp chopped fresh parsley (optional)
- * Salt to taste

Instructions for the Baked Salmon:

- Preheat the oven to 375°F (190°C).
- Place salmon fillets on a baking sheet lined with parchment paper.
- Drizzle olive oil and lemon juice over the salmon.
- Sprinkle garlic powder, dried dill, salt, and pepper.
- Place lemon slices on top of the salmon fillets.
- Bake in the preheated oven for 15-20 minutes, until the salmon flakes easily.

Steamed Veggies Variant:

- In a steamer basket, add broccoli, baby carrots, and snap peas.
- Steam the vegetables for 7-10 minutes until tender.
- Toss the steamed veggies with olive oil, lemon zest, salt, and pepper before serving.

Brown Rice Variant:

- Rinse the brown rice under cold water.

- In a medium saucepan, bring 2 cups of water to a boil.

- Add the rinsed brown rice and a pinch of salt.

- Reduce heat to low, cover, and simmer for 35-40 minutes until the water is absorbed and rice is tender.

- Fluff the rice with a fork and stir in fresh parsley if using.

Baked chicken with green beans/quinoa

Prep time
15 mins

Cook Time
30 mins

Servings
2 per.

Calorie
400-450 kcal

For the Chicken:

- **2** boneless, skinless chicken breasts
- **1** tbsp olive oil (15 ml)
- **1** tsp garlic powder (5 ml)
- **1** tsp paprika (5 ml)
- **1/2** tsp salt (2.5 ml)
- **1/4** tsp black pepper (1.25 ml)
- **1** lemon, sliced
- ***** Fresh parsley (optional)

For the Green Beans:

- **2** cups fresh green beans, trimmed (about 200 grams)
- **1** tsp olive oil (5 ml)
- **1/4** tsp salt (1.25 ml)
- **1/4** tsp black pepper (1.25 ml)
- **1/2** tsp garlic powder (2.5 ml)

For the Quinoa:

- **1/2** cup quinoa (90 grams)
- **1** cup water (240 ml)
- **1/4** tsp salt (1.25 ml)

Chicken Preparation:

- Preheat your oven to 400°F (200°C).

- In a small bowl, mix together olive oil, garlic powder, paprika, salt, and pepper.

- Rub the chicken breasts with the spice mixture, ensuring they are well-coated.

- Place the chicken breasts in a baking dish and arrange lemon slices on top.

- Bake in the preheated oven for 25-30 minutes, or until the internal temperature reaches 165°F (74°C).

- Once done, let the chicken rest for 5 minutes before serving. Garnish with fresh parsley if desired.

Green Beans Variant:

- While the chicken is baking, prepare the green beans.

- In a bowl, toss the green beans with olive oil, salt, pepper, and garlic powder.

- Spread the green beans on a baking sheet in a single layer.

- Bake in the oven for 15-20 minutes, or until tender and slightly crispy.

Quinoa Variant:

- While the chicken is baking, rinse the quinoa under cold water.

- In a medium saucepan, bring water and salt to a boil.

- Add the quinoa, reduce the heat to low, cover, and simmer for 15 minutes or until the water is absorbed and the quinoa is tender.

- Fluff the quinoa with a fork before serving, then serve.

Baked cod with sweet potato

Prep time 15 mins	Cook Time 30 mins	Servings 2 per.	Calorie 300 kcal

Ingredients:

- **2** cod fillets (about 4 oz each)
- **1** large sweet potato
- **1** tbsp olive oil
- **1** tsp garlic powder
- **1** tsp paprika
- **1** tsp dried thyme
- **1/2** tsp black pepper
- **1/4** tsp salt
- **1** lemon (sliced)
- * Fresh parsley for garnish (optional)

Instructions for for Preparing:

- Preheat your oven to 400°F (200°C).

- Peel and cut the sweet potato into 1/2-inch thick slices.

- In a bowl, toss the sweet potato slices with 1/2 tbsp olive oil, 1/2 tsp garlic powder, 1/2 tsp paprika, 1/2 tsp dried thyme, 1/4 tsp black pepper, and 1/8 tsp salt.

- Spread the sweet potato slices on a baking sheet lined with parchment paper.

- Bake the sweet potato slices in the preheated oven for 15 minutes.

Prepare the Cod:

- While the sweet potato is baking, prepare the cod fillets.

- In a small bowl, mix 1/2 tbsp olive oil, 1/2 tsp garlic powder, 1/2 tsp paprika, 1/2 tsp dried thyme, 1/4 tsp black pepper, and 1/8 tsp salt.

- Brush the seasoning mixture evenly over both sides of the cod fillets.

Bake the Cod:

- After the sweet potato has baked for 15 minutes, remove the baking sheet from the oven.

- Move the sweet potato slices to one side of the baking sheet and place the cod fillets on the other side.

- Top each cod fillet with a slice of lemon.

- Return the baking sheet to the oven and bake for an additional 15-20 minutes, or until the cod is opaque and flakes easily with a fork, and the sweet potatoes are tender.

Serve:

- Plate the cod fillets and sweet potato slices.

- Garnish with fresh parsley and additional lemon slices if desired.

Turkey stir-fry with brown rice

Prep time
15 mins

Cook Time
30 mins

Servings
2 per.

Calorie
450 kcal

Turkey Stir-Fry:

- **1/2** lb (225 g) ground turkey breast
- **1** tbsp olive oil
- **1** medium onion, chopped
- **2** cloves garlic, minced
- **1** red bell pepper, sliced
- **1** yellow bell pepper, sliced
- **1** cup broccoli florets
- **1** cup snap peas
- **1** medium carrot, julienned

- **2** tbsp low-sodium soy sauce
- **1** tbsp hoisin sauce
- **1** tbsp rice vinegar
- **1** tsp sesame oil
- **1/4** tsp black pepper
- **1/4** tsp red pepper flakes (optional)
- **1** tbsp sesame seeds (optional for garnish)
- **2** green onions, sliced (optional for garnish)

Brown Rice:

- **1** cup brown rice
- **2** cups water

Instructions for Brown Rice:

- In a medium pot, bring 2 cups of water to a boil.
- Add 1 cup of brown rice, reduce heat to low, cover, and simmer for about 25-30 minutes until the water is absorbed and rice is tender. Fluff with a fork.

Instructions for Turkey Stir-Fry:

- Heat 1 Tbsp of olive oil in a large skillet or wok over medium-high heat.
- Add chopped onion and cook for 2-3 minutes until translucent.
- Add minced garlic and cook for another 30 seconds.

2.
- Add ground turkey breast, cook and crumble until fully cooked (about 5-7 minutes).
- Add red and yellow bell peppers, broccoli, snap peas, and carrot. Stir-fry for about 5-7 minutes until vegetables are tender-crisp.
- In a small bowl, mix low-sodium soy sauce, hoisin sauce, rice vinegar, sesame oil, black pepper, and red pepper flakes (if using).
- Pour the sauce mixture over the turkey and vegetables. Stir to combine and cook for another 2-3 minutes until everything is well-coated and heated through.
- Divide the cooked brown rice between two plates & Top with the turkey stir-fry.
- Garnish with sesame seeds and sliced green onions if desired & serve.

Grilled shrimp with mixed greens

Prep time
15 mins

Cook Time
6 mins

Servings
2 per.

Calorie
320 kcal

Shrimp Marinade:

- **12** large shrimp, peeled and deveined
- **2** tbsp olive oil
- **1** tbsp lemon juice
- **1** clove garlic, minced
- **1/2** tsp paprika
- **1/4** tsp black pepper
- **1/4** tsp salt

Dressing:

- **2** tbsp olive oil
- **1** tbsp balsamic vinegar
- **1** tsp Dijon mustard

Salad:

- **4** cups mixed greens (arugula, spinach, romaine)
- **1/2** cup cherry tomatoes, halved
- **1/4** cup red onion, thinly sliced
- **1/4** cup cucumber, sliced
- **1/4** cup bell pepper, sliced
- **1/4** cup feta cheese, crumbled

- **1** tsp honey
- ***** Salt & pepper to taste

Instructions for Marinate the Shrimp:

- In a medium bowl, combine olive oil, lemon juice, minced garlic, paprika, black pepper, and salt.

- Add the shrimp to the bowl, ensuring they are well coated with the marinade.

- Cover and refrigerate for at least 30 minutes.

Prepare the Salad:

- While the shrimp is marinating, prepare the mixed greens and other salad ingredients.

- In a large salad bowl, combine mixed greens, cherry tomatoes, red onion, cucumber, bell pepper, and feta cheese.

- In a small bowl, whisk together olive oil, balsamic vinegar, Dijon mustard, honey, salt, and pepper until well combined.

Prepare the Shrimp & Salad:

- Preheat the grill to medium-high heat.

- Thread the shrimp onto skewers (if using wooden skewers, soak them in water for 30 minutes beforehand to prevent burning).

- Grill the shrimp for 2-3 minutes on each side, or until they are opaque and cooked through

- Remove the shrimp from the skewers and place them on top of the mixed greens.

- Drizzle the dressing over the salad and toss gently to combine..

Grilled chicken with quinoa/sweet potato

Prep time	Cook Time	Servings	Calorie
15 mins	30 mins	2 per.	400-450 kcal

For Grilled Chicken:

- **2** boneless, skinless chicken breasts (about 6 oz each)
- **2** tbsp olive oil
- **2** cloves garlic, minced
- **1** tbsp lemon juice
- **1** tsp dried oregano
- **1** tsp dried thyme
- **1/2** tsp salt
- **1/4** tsp black pepper

For Sweet Potato Variant:

- **2** medium sweet potatoes
- **1** tbsp olive oil
- **1/2** tsp paprika
- **1/2** tsp garlic powder
- **1/2** tsp salt
- **1/4** tsp black pepper

For Quinoa Variant:

- **1** cup quinoa
- **2** cups low-sodium chicken broth or water
- **1/2** cup cherry tomatoes, halved
- **1/2** cup cucumber, diced
- **1/4** cup red onion, finely chopped
- **2** tbsp fresh parsley, chopped
- **1** tbsp olive oil
- **1** tbsp lemon juice
- ***** Salt and pepper to taste

Chicken Preparation:

- In a small bowl, mix olive oil, minced garlic, lemon juice, oregano, thyme, salt, and black pepper.

- Place the chicken breasts in a resealable plastic bag or shallow dish and pour the marinade over the chicken.

- Marinate in the refrigerator for at least 30 minutes, or up to 2 hours for better flavor.

- Preheat the grill to medium-high heat.

- Grill the chicken breasts for about 6-7 minutes per side, or until the internal temperature reaches 165°F (75°C).

- Let the chicken rest for a few minutes before serving.

Quinoa Variant:

- Rinse the quinoa under cold water.

- In a medium saucepan, bring the chicken broth or water to a boil.

- Add the quinoa, reduce the heat to low, cover, and simmer for about 15 minutes, or until the quinoa is tender and the liquid is absorbed.

- Fluff with a fork.

- In a large bowl, combine the cooked quinoa, cherry tomatoes, cucumber, red onion, and parsley.

- Drizzle with olive oil and lemon juice.

- Season with salt and pepper to taste.

Sweet Potato Variant:

- Preheat the oven to 400°F (200°C).

- Peel and cut the sweet potatoes into 1-inch cubes.

- In a large bowl, toss the sweet potatoes with olive oil, paprika, garlic powder, salt, and black pepper.

- Spread the sweet potatoes in a single layer on a baking sheet.

- Roast for about 25-30 minutes, or until tender and slightly crispy, stirring halfway through the cooking time.

Grilled cod with quinoa

Prep time 15 mins	Cook Time 30 mins	Servings 2 per.	Calorie 400 kcal

For the Grilled Cod:

- **2** cod fillets (about 6 ounces each)
- **1** tbsp olive oil
- **1** tbsp lemon juice
- **1** clove garlic, minced
- **1** tsp dried thyme
- * Salt and pepper to taste

For the Quinoa:

- **1** cup quinoa, rinsed
- **2** cups low-sodium vegetable broth or water
- **1** tbsp olive oil
- **1** small onion, finely chopped
- **1** bell pepper, finely chopped
- **1** clove garlic, minced
- **1** tsp ground cumin
- **1/2** tsp ground coriander
- * Salt and pepper to taste
- **1/4** cup chopped fresh parsley

Instructions for Grilled Cod:

- Marinate the Cod: In a small bowl, combine olive oil, lemon juice, minced garlic, dried thyme, salt, and pepper. Brush this mixture over the cod fillets. Let them marinate for at least 10 minutes.

- Preheat the Grill: Preheat your grill to medium-high heat.

- Grill the Cod: Place the cod fillets on the grill. Cook for about 4-5 minutes on each side, or until the fish flakes easily with a fork.

Instructions for the Quinoa:

- In a medium saucepan, bring the vegetable broth or water to a boil. Add the rinsed quinoa, reduce heat to low, cover, and simmer for about 15 minutes, or until the quinoa is tender and the liquid is absorbed. Fluff with a fork.

- While the quinoa is cooking, heat olive oil in a large skillet over medium heat. Add the chopped onion and bell pepper, & sauté for about 5 minutes, until they are soft.

- Add Garlic and Spices: Stir in the minced garlic, ground cumin, and ground coriander. Cook for another 2 minutes until fragrant.

- Add the cooked quinoa to the skillet with the vegetables. Stir well to combine. Season with salt and pepper to taste.

- Stir in the chopped fresh parsley just before serving.

- Serve the grilled cod fillets alongside the quinoa.

Grilled tilapia with asparagus

Prep time
10 mins

Cook Time
15 mins

Servings
2 per.

Calorie
300 kcal

Ingredients:

- **2** tilapia fillets (about 6 oz each)
- **1** bunch of asparagus (about 1 lb)
- **2** tbsp olive oil
- **1** tsp garlic powder

- **1** tsp onion powder
- **1** tsp paprika
- **1** lemon, sliced
- ***** Salt and pepper to taste

Instructions for the Tilapia:

1.
- Preheat your grill to medium-high heat.
- Rinse the tilapia fillets under cold water and pat them dry with a paper towel.
- In a small bowl, mix together the garlic powder, onion powder, paprika, salt, and pepper.
- Rub the tilapia fillets with 1 tbsp of olive oil and then sprinkle the spice mixture evenly over both sides of the fillets.

Instructions for the Asparagus:

2.
- Rinse the asparagus under cold water and trim the tough ends.
- Toss the asparagus with the remaining 1 tbsp of olive oil, and season with salt and pepper.

Grill the Tilapia and Asparagus:

3.
- Place the tilapia fillets and asparagus directly on the preheated grill.
- Grill the tilapia for about 4-5 minutes per side, until the fish is opaque and flakes easily with a fork.
- Grill the asparagus for about 8-10 minutes, turning occasionally, until they are tender and have nice grill marks.

3.
- Remove the tilapia and asparagus from the grill and transfer them to serving plates.
- Squeeze fresh lemon juice over the tilapia and asparagus & serve.

Grill the Tilapia and Asparagus:

3.
- Place the tilapia fillets and asparagus directly on the preheated grill.
- Grill the tilapia for about 4-5 minutes per side, until the fish is opaque and flakes easily with a fork.
- Grill the asparagus for about 8-10 minutes, turning occasionally, until they are tender and have nice grill marks.
- Remove the tilapia and asparagus from the grill and transfer them to serving plates.
- Squeeze fresh lemon juice over the tilapia and asparagus & serve.

Grilled steak with green beans

Prep time	Cook Time	Servings	Calorie
15 mins	15 mins	2 per.	320 kcal

Ingredients:

- **2** (4 oz) lean beef steaks
- **1** lb fresh green beans, trimmed
- **1** tbsp olive oil
- **2** tsp minced garlic
- **1** tsp lemon zest

- **1** tbsp fresh lemon juice
- **1** tbsp fresh parsley, chopped
- * Salt and pepper to taste
- * Cooking spray

Instructions for the Steaks:

1.
- Season the steaks with salt and pepper on both sides.
- Let them rest at room temperature for 15-20 minutes.

Instructions for the Green Beans:

2.
- In a large bowl, toss the green beans with olive oil, garlic, salt, and pepper.

Grill the Steaks & Green Beans:

3.
- Preheat the grill to medium-high heat.
- Spray the grill grates with cooking spray to prevent sticking.
- Grill the steaks for about 4-5 minutes on each side, or until they reach your desired level of doneness.
- Remove the steaks from the grill and let them rest for 5 minutes before serving.
- While the steaks are resting, place the green beans on the grill.
- Grill for 3-4 minutes, turning occasionally, until they are tender-crisp and slightly charred.

Finish the Green Beans & Serve:

4.
- Transfer the green beans to a serving bowl.
- Toss with lemon zest, lemon juice, and chopped parsley.
- Plate the steaks with a side of grilled green beans.

Grilled turkey burger with salad

Prep time
15 mins

Cook Time
12 mins

Servings
2 per.

Calorie
450 kcal

For the Salad:

- **4** cups mixed salad greens
- **1** cup cherry tomatoes, halved
- **1** small cucumber, sliced
- **1/4** cup red onion, thinly sliced
- **1/4** cup low-fat feta cheese, crumbled
- **2** tbsp balsamic vinaigrette dressing

For the Turkey Burger:

- **1** lb ground turkey
- **1** small onion, finely chopped
- **2** cloves garlic, minced
- **2** tbsp (tablespoon) whole-wheat bread crumbs

- **1** egg white
- **1** tbsp olive oil
- **1** tsp (teaspoon) dried oregano
- **1** tsp dried basil
- **1/2** tsp salt
- **1/2** tsp black pepper

Instructions for the Turkey Burgers:

1.

- Combine Ingredients: In a large bowl, mix the ground turkey, chopped onion, minced garlic, bread crumbs, egg white, olive oil, oregano, basil, salt, and black pepper until well combined.
- Form Patties: Divide the mixture into two equal portions and shape into patties.
- Preheat Grill: Preheat the grill to medium-high heat.

Instructions for the Salad:

2.

- Prepare Vegetables: Rinse and chop the salad greens, cherry tomatoes, cucumber, and red onion.
- Assemble Salad: In a large salad bowl, combine the mixed greens, cherry tomatoes, cucumber, red onion, and feta cheese.
- Add Dressing: Drizzle with balsamic vinaigrette dressing and toss to coat.

Cooking& Serving:

- Grill Patties: Place the turkey patties on the preheated grill. Cook for about 5-6 minutes on each side, or until the internal temperature reaches 165°F (74°C) and the patties are cooked through.
- Rest: Remove the patties from the grill and let them rest for a few minutes before serving.
- Plate Burgers: Serve each turkey burger on a whole-grain bun or over a bed of salad greens, if desired.
- Side Salad: Serve the prepared salad on the side.

Stuffed bell peppers

Prep time
20 mins

Cook Time
45 mins

Servings
2 per.

Calorie
300 kcal

Ingredients:

- **4** large bell peppers (any color)
- **1** cup quinoa, cooked
- **1** can (15 oz) black beans, rinsed and drained
- **1** cup corn kernels (fresh, frozen, or canned)
- **1** small onion, finely chopped
- **2** cloves garlic, minced
- **1** cup cherry tomatoes, halved
- **1/2** cup low-fat shredded cheese (optional)
- **1/4** cup fresh cilantro, chopped
- **1** tbsp olive oil
- **1** tsp cumin
- **1** tsp smoked paprika
- * Salt and pepper to taste
- **1/2** cup low-sodium vegetable broth

Instructions for for Preparing:

1.
- Preheat your oven to 375°F (190°C).
- Cut the tops off the bell peppers and remove the seeds and membranes.
- Lightly brush the insides with a bit of olive oil and place them in a baking dish.

Cook the filling:

2.
- Heat 1 Tbsp of olive oil in a large pan over medium heat.
- Add the chopped onion and cook until translucent, about 5 minutes.
- Add the minced garlic, cumin, and smoked paprika, and cook for another 1-2 minutes.

Combine ingredients:

3.
- Add the cooked quinoa, black beans, corn, and cherry tomatoes to the pan. Stir well to combine.

3.

- Season with salt and pepper to taste.

- Stir in the chopped cilantro.

Stuff the bell peppers:

4.

- Spoon the quinoa mixture into the prepared bell peppers, filling them to the top.

- Pour the low-sodium vegetable broth into the bottom of the baking dish to keep the peppers moist during baking.

Bake:

5.

- Cover the baking dish with foil and bake in the preheated oven for 30 minutes.

- Remove the foil, sprinkle the optional shredded cheese on top of each pepper, and bake for an additional 10-15 minutes, or until the peppers are tender and the cheese is melted and bubbly.

Beef stir-fry with vegetables

Prep time
15 mins

Cook Time
15 mins

Servings
2 per.

Calorie
350 kcal

For the stir-fry:

- **8** oz lean beef (sirloin or tenderloin), thinly sliced
- **1** tbsp olive oil
- **1** cup broccoli florets
- **1** bell pepper, sliced
- **1** carrot, thinly sliced
- **1/2** cup snap peas
- **1** small onion, thinly sliced
- **1/2** cup low-sodium beef broth
- **1** tbsp cornstarch
- **1/2** tsp black pepper
- **1/4** cup fresh basil, chopped (optional for garnish)

For the marinade:

- **2** tbsp low-sodium soy sauce
- **1** tbsp rice vinegar
- **1** tbsp honey
- **1** tsp sesame oil
- **1** garlic clove, minced
- **1** tsp fresh ginger, grated

Instructions for the Marinade:

- In a small bowl, mix together 2 Tbsp low-sodium soy sauce, 1 Tbsp rice vinegar, 1 Tbsp honey, 1 tsp sesame oil, minced garlic, and grated ginger.

- Place the thinly sliced beef in a bowl and pour the marinade over it. Let it marinate for at least 10 minutes while you prepare the vegetables.

Cook the Beef:

- In a large non-stick skillet or wok, heat 1 Tbsp olive oil over medium-high heat.

- Add the marinated beef and cook for about 3-4 minutes until it's browned. Remove the beef from the skillet and set aside.

Cook the Vegetables:

- Wash and cut the broccoli florets, bell pepper, carrot, snap peas, and onion.

- In the same skillet, add the onion, broccoli, bell pepper, carrot, and snap peas. Stir-fry for about 5-6 minutes until the vegetables are tender but still crisp.

- Return the beef to the skillet with the vegetables. Stir to combine.

Prepare the Sauce:

- In a small bowl, mix 1/2 cup low-sodium beef broth with 1 Tbsp cornstarch until smooth. Pour this mixture into the skillet.

- Stir well and cook for another 2-3 minutes until the sauce thickens.

- Season with 1/2 tsp black pepper &g arnish with fresh basil if desired.

Beef and broccoli stir-fry

Prep time 10 mins	Cook Time 10 mins	Servings 2 per.	Calorie 250 kcal

Ingredients:

- **200** g lean beef sirloin, thinly sliced
- **2** cups broccoli florets

- **1** red bell pepper, sliced
- **1** small onion, thinly sliced

- **2** cloves garlic, minced
- **1** tbsp low-sodium soy sauce
- **1** tbsp oyster sauce
- **1** tbsp cornstarch
- **1/4** cup low-sodium beef broth

- **1** tbsp olive oil
- **1** tsp sesame oil
- **1** tsp grated ginger
- **1/4** tsp black pepper
- **1** tbsp water

Instructions for Preparing:

1.
- In a small bowl, mix the cornstarch with 1 tbsp water to make a slurry. Set aside.
- In another small bowl, mix the soy sauce, oyster sauce, beef broth, and black pepper.

Cooking:

2.
- Heat olive oil in a large pan or wok over medium-high heat.
- Add the sliced beef and cook for 2-3 minutes until browned. Remove from the pan and set aside.
- In the same pan, add garlic and ginger, and cook for 1 minute until fragrant.
- Add the broccoli, red bell pepper, and onion. Stir-fry for 3-4 minutes until the vegetables are tender-crisp.
- Return the beef to the pan. Stir in the soy sauce mixture and the cornstarch slurry.
- Cook for an additional 2-3 minutes until the sauce thickens and everything is well combined.
- Drizzle with sesame oil and give a final stir.
- Serve hot over a bed of brown rice or quinoa for a complete meal.

Spaghetti marinara & turkey meatballs

Prep time 15 mins	Cook Time 30 mins	Servings 2 per.	Calorie 450 kcal

For the Marinara Sauce:

- **1** tbsp olive oil
- **1** small onion, finely chopped
- **3** garlic cloves, minced
- **1** can (14.5 oz) diced tomatoes, no salt added
- **1** can (8 oz) tomato sauce, no salt added
- **1** tsp dried basil
- **1** tsp dried oregano
- **1/2** tsp black pepper
- **1/4** tsp red pepper flakes (optional)

For the Turkey Meatballs:

- **1/2** lb ground turkey breast
- **1/4** cup whole wheat breadcrumbs
- **1/4** cup grated Parmesan cheese
- **1** egg, lightly beaten
- **1** tbsp fresh parsley, finely chopped (or 1 tsp dried parsley)
- **1/2** tsp garlic powder
- **1/2** tsp onion powder
- **1/4** tsp black pepper

For the Spaghetti:

- **4** oz whole wheat spaghetti

Instructions for Marinara Sauce:

- Heat olive oil in a large saucepan over medium heat.
- Add chopped onion and sauté until translucent, about 5 minutes.
- Add minced garlic and sauté for an additional 1-2 minutes.
- Stir in diced tomatoes and tomato sauce.
- Add basil, oregano, black pepper, and red pepper flakes (if using).
- Simmer the sauce for about 20 minutes, stirring occasionally.e vegetables.

Instructions for Turkey Meatballs:

- Preheat oven to 375°F (190°C) and line a baking sheet with parchment paper.
- In a large bowl, combine ground turkey, breadcrumbs, Parmesan cheese, beaten egg, parsley, garlic powder, onion powder, and black pepper.
- Mix well until all ingredients are evenly combined.
- Form the mixture into small meatballs, about 1 inch in diameter, and place them on the prepared baking sheet.
- Bake for 15-20 minutes, or until the meatballs are cooked through and golden brown.

Prepare the Spaghetti:

- While the meatballs are baking, cook the spaghetti according to the package instructions.

- Drain and set aside.

- Combine the cooked meatballs with the marinara sauce.

- Serve the meatballs and sauce over the cooked spaghetti.

- Garnish with additional parsley and Parmesan cheese if desired.

Chicken and vegetable stir-fry

Prep time 15 mins	Cook Time 15 mins	Servings 2 per.	Calorie 300 kcal

Chicken and Marinade:

- **1** large chicken breast (about 6 oz), thinly sliced
- **1** tbsp low-sodium soy sauce
- **1** tbsp rice vinegar
- **1** tsp sesame oil
- **1** clove garlic, minced
- **1/2** tsp ginger, grated

Sauce:

- **2** tbsp low-sodium soy sauce
- **1** tbsp hoisin sauce
- **1** tsp cornstarch
- **1/4** cup water

Vegetables:

- **1** cup broccoli florets
- **1** medium carrot, thinly sliced
- **1** red bell pepper, thinly sliced
- **1/2** cup snap peas
- **1/2** small onion, thinly sliced
- **1** tbsp olive oil

Optional Garnish:

- **1** tbsp sesame seeds
- **2** green onions, thinly sliced

Marinate the Chicken:

- In a bowl, combine 1 Tbsp soy sauce, 1 Tbsp rice vinegar, 1 tsp sesame oil, minced garlic, and grated ginger.

- Add the thinly sliced chicken breast and mix well. Let it marinate for at least 10 minutes while you prepare the vegetables.

Prepare the Vegetables:

- Wash and cut the broccoli into small florets.

- Peel and thinly slice the carrot.

- Slice the red bell pepper and onion thinly.

Make the Sauce:

- In a small bowl, whisk together 2 Tbsp soy sauce, 1 Tbsp hoisin sauce, 1 tsp cornstarch, and 1/4 cup water until the cornstarch is fully dissolved.

Cook:

- Heat 1 Tbsp olive oil in a large skillet or wok over medium-high heat.

- Add the marinated chicken to the skillet and stir-fry for about 5 minutes, or until the chicken is cooked through and slightly browned.

- Remove the chicken from the skillet and set aside.

- In the same skillet, add a little more olive oil if needed.

- Add the sliced onion and stir-fry for about 1-2 minutes until it starts to soften.

- Add the broccoli, carrot, bell pepper, and snap peas.

- Stir-fry the vegetables for about 5-7 minutes, or until they are tender-crisp.

Combine and Finish:

- Return the cooked chicken to the skillet with the vegetables.

- Pour the prepared sauce over the chicken and vegetables.

- Stir well to coat everything in the sauce and cook for an additional 2-3 minutes until the sauce has thickened slightly.

- Divide the stir-fry between two plates &garnish with green onions if desired.

Shrimp stir-fry with brown rice

Prep time
15 mins

Cook Time
40 mins

Servings
2 per.

Calorie
450 kcal

For the Shrimp Stir-Fry:

- **1/2** lb (225g) shrimp, peeled and deveined
- **1** cup mixed vegetables (such as bell peppers, broccoli, and snap peas)
- **2** cloves garlic, minced
- **1** inch ginger, minced
- **1** tbsp low-sodium soy sauce
- **1** tbsp olive oil
- **1** tsp sesame oil
- **1** tsp cornstarch
- **2** tbsp water

For the Brown Rice:

- **1** cup brown rice
- **2** cups water

Prepare the Brown Rice:

1.
- Rinse the brown rice under cold water.
- In a medium saucepan, bring 2 cups of water to a boil.
- Add the rice, reduce the heat to low, cover, and simmer for about 45 minutes, or until the rice is tender and the water is absorbed.
- Fluff with a fork and set aside.

Prepare the Shrimp Stir-Fry:

2.
- In a small bowl, mix the cornstarch and water to create a slurry. Set aside.
- Heat the olive oil in a large skillet or wok over medium-high heat.
- Add the minced garlic and ginger, and sauté for about 30 seconds until fragrant.
- Add the shrimp and cook for 2-3 minutes on each side, until pink and cooked through. Remove from the skillet and set aside.
- In the same skillet, add the mixed vegetables and stir-fry for 3-4 minutes, until they are tender-crisp.
- Return the shrimp to the skillet, add the soy sauce, and drizzle with sesame oil.

2.

- Stir in the cornstarch slurry and cook for another 1-2 minutes until the sauce thickens.

Serve:

3.

- Divide the brown rice between two plates.

- Top with the shrimp stir-fry mixture & serve.

Shrimp and quinoa bowl

Prep time
15 mins

Cook Time
20 mins

Servings
2 per.

Calorie
450 kcal

For the Quinoa:

- **1** cup quinoa, rinsed

- **2** cups low-sodium vegetable broth

- **1** tbsp olive oil

- **1/2** tsp salt

For the Shrimp:

- **12** large shrimp, peeled and deveined

- **1** tbsp olive oil

- **2** cloves garlic, minced

- **1** tsp paprika

- **1/2** tsp cumin

- **1/4** tsp black pepper

- **1/4** tsp salt

For the Vegetables:

- **1** cup cherry tomatoes, halved

- **1** cup cucumber, diced

- **1/2** red onion, finely chopped

- **1/2** cup parsley, chopped

- **1** avocado, diced

- **2** tbsp lemon juice

- **1** tbsp olive oil

- **1/4** tsp salt

- **1/4** tsp black pepper

Preparing the Quinoa:

1.

- In a medium saucepan, heat 1 tbsp olive oil over medium heat.

- Add the rinsed quinoa and toast for about 2 minutes, stirring occasionally.

1.

- Pour in the low-sodium vegetable broth and add 1/2 tsp salt.

- Bring to a boil, then reduce the heat to low, cover, and simmer for about 15 minutes, or until the quinoa is tender and the liquid is absorbed.

- Fluff with a fork and set aside.

Cooking the Shrimp:

2.

- In a medium bowl, combine the shrimp, 1 tbsp olive oil, minced garlic, paprika, cumin, black pepper, and 1/4 tsp salt. Mix well to coat the shrimp evenly.

- Heat a large skillet over medium-high heat. Add the seasoned shrimp and cook for about 2-3 minutes on each side, or until the shrimp are pink and opaque. Remove from heat.

Assembling the Vegetables:

3.

- In a large bowl, combine the cherry tomatoes, cucumber, red onion, parsley, and avocado.

- Drizzle with lemon juice and 1 tbsp olive oil. Season with 1/4 tsp salt and 1/4 tsp black pepper. Toss gently to combine.

Assembling the Bowl:

4.

- Divide the cooked quinoa equally between two bowls.

- Top each bowl with half of the vegetable mixture.

- Add 6 cooked shrimp to each bowl.

- Garnish with extra parsley or a lemon wedge, if desired.

Turkey meatballs with zucchini

Prep time	Cook Time	Servings	Calorie
15 mins	20 mins	2 per.	250 kcal

Ingredients:

- **200** grams ground turkey
- **1** medium zucchini, grated
- **1** small onion, finely chopped
- **1** garlic clove, minced
- **1** egg
- **2** tbsp whole wheat breadcrumbs

- **1** tbsp fresh parsley, chopped
- **1** tsp dried oregano
- **1/2** tsp salt
- **1/4** tsp black pepper
- **1** tbsp olive oil

Prepare the Ingredients:

1.
- Grate the zucchini and squeeze out excess moisture using a clean kitchen towel.
- Finely chop the onion and mince the garlic.

Mix the Meatballs:

2.
- In a large bowl, combine the ground turkey, grated zucchini, chopped onion, minced garlic, egg, whole wheat breadcrumbs, chopped parsley, dried oregano, salt, and black pepper.
- Mix thoroughly until all ingredients are well combined.

Form the Meatballs:

3.
- Shape the mixture into small meatballs, about 1 inch in diameter. You should have approximately 8-10 meatballs.

Cook the Meatballs:

4.
- Heat the olive oil in a large skillet over medium heat.
- Add the meatballs to the skillet and cook for about 10 minutes, turning occasionally, until all sides are browned.
- Reduce the heat to low, cover the skillet, and let the meatballs cook for an additional 10 minutes or until cooked through.

06

— Chapter —

Soups & Stews

Vegetable Lentil Soup

Prep time
15 mins

Cook Time
40 mins

Servings
2 per.

Calorie
250 kcal

Ingredients:

- **1** cup lentils
- **1** medium onion, chopped
- **2** cloves garlic, minced
- **2** carrots, chopped
- **2** celery stalks, chopped
- **1** bell pepper, chopped
- **1** zucchini, chopped
- **1** cup spinach, chopped
- **1** can (14.5 oz) diced tomatoes, undrained
- **4** cups low-sodium vegetable broth

- **1** tsp olive oil
- **1** tsp dried thyme
- **1** tsp dried oregano
- **1** tsp cumin
- **1/2** tsp black pepper
- **1/2** tsp turmeric
- **1/4** tsp salt (optional)
- **2** tbsp lemon juice
- ***** Fresh parsley, chopped (for garnish)

Prepare the Lentils & Sauté Vegetables:

- Rinse the lentils under cold water and set aside.
- In a large pot, heat the olive oil over medium heat.
- Add the chopped onion and garlic, and sauté until they are translucent (about 5 minutes).
- Add the chopped carrots, celery, and bell pepper to the pot.
- Sauté for another 5 minutes until the vegetables begin to soften.

- Stir in the thyme, oregano, cumin, black pepper, and turmeric.
- Cook for 1 minute to release the flavors of the spices.
- Add the rinsed lentils and vegetable broth to the pot.
- Bring the mixture to a boil, then reduce the heat to a simmer.
- Let the soup simmer for about 25 minutes, or until the lentils are tender.

3.
- Stir in the diced tomatoes (with juice), zucchini, and spinach.
- Simmer for an additional 10 minutes.
- Stir in the lemon juice and adjust seasoning with salt if needed.
- Ladle the soup into bowls, garnish with chopped parsley, and serve hot.

Gazpacho

Prep time
15 mins

Cook Time
40 mins

Servings
2 per.

Calorie
250 kcal

Ingredients:

- **4** large ripe tomatoes, chopped
- **1** cucumber, peeled and chopped
- **1** red bell pepper, seeded and chopped
- **1** green bell pepper, seeded and chopped
- **1** small red onion, chopped
- **2** cloves garlic, minced
- **2** cups low-sodium tomato juice
- **3** tbsp extra virgin olive oil

- **2** tbsp red wine vinegar
- **1** tsp salt
- **1/2** tsp black pepper
- **1/2** tsp ground cumin
- **1/4** cup fresh cilantro, chopped (optional)
- **1/4** cup fresh basil, chopped (optional)
- ***** Lemon wedges for serving

Instructions:

1.
- In a large bowl, combine the chopped tomatoes, cucumber, red and green bell peppers, and red onion.
- Transfer half of the vegetable mixture to a blender.
- Add the minced garlic, 1 cup of tomato juice, and blend until smooth.
- Pour the blended mixture back into the bowl with the remaining chopped vegetables.

2.
- Stir in the extra virgin olive oil, red wine vinegar, salt, black pepper, and ground cumin.
- Mix thoroughly to ensure the seasonings are well distributed.

3.

- Cover the bowl and refrigerate for at least 2 hours to allow the flavors to meld. Simmer for an additional 10 minutes.

- Before serving, stir the gazpacho well.

- Ladle into bowls and garnish with fresh cilantro and basil if desired.

- Serve with lemon wedges on the side.

Minestrone Soup

Prep time
15 mins

Cook Time
30 mins

Servings
2 per.

Calorie
250 kcal

Ingredients:

- **1** tbsp olive oil

- **1/2** medium onion, diced

- **1** small carrot, diced

- **1** celery stalk, diced

- **2** garlic cloves, minced

- **1** small zucchini, diced

- **1/2** cup green beans, cut into 1-inch pieces

- **1** can (14.5 oz) diced tomatoes, no salt added

- **3** cups low-sodium vegetable broth

- **1/2** cup canned cannellini beans, drained and rinsed

- **1/4** cup whole wheat pasta (small shapes like ditalini or elbow)

- **1/2** tsp dried oregano

- **1/2** tsp dried basil

- **1/4** tsp black pepper

- **1/4** tsp salt (optional)

- **1** cup fresh spinach, chopped

- **1** tbsp fresh parsley, chopped

- **1** tbsp grated Parmesan cheese (optional, for garnish)

Instructions:

- In a large pot, heat the olive oil over medium heat.

- Add the diced onion, carrot, and celery to the pot. Sauté for about 5 minutes until the vegetables are softened.

- Stir in the minced garlic and diced zucchini, cooking for another 2 minutes.

2.

- Add the green beans and diced tomatoes to the pot, stirring to combine.

- Pour in the vegetable broth, and add the dried oregano, dried basil, black pepper, and salt (if using). Bring the mixture to a boil.

- Once boiling, reduce the heat to a simmer. Stir in the cannellini beans and whole wheat pasta. Simmer for about 10 minutes or until the pasta is tender.

3.

- Stir in the chopped spinach and let it cook for another 2 minutes until wilted.

- Ladle the soup into bowls, garnish with fresh parsley and grated Parmesan cheese if desired.

Spinach and White Bean Soup

Prep time	Cook Time	Servings	Calorie
10 mins	20 mins	2 per.	250 kcal

Ingredients:

- **1** tbsp olive oil
- **1** small onion, finely chopped
- **2** cloves garlic, minced
- **1** carrot, diced
- **1** celery stalk, diced
- **1** can (15 oz) white beans, drained & rinsed
- **4** cups fresh spinach, roughly chopped

- **4** cups low-sodium vegetable broth
- **1** tsp dried thyme
- **1** tsp dried basil
- **1/2** tsp salt (optional)
- **1/4** tsp black pepper
- **1** tbsp lemon juice (optional, for added flavor)

Instructions:

1.

- In a large pot, heat the olive oil over medium heat.

- Add the chopped onion, garlic, carrot, and celery. Sauté for about 5 minutes, until the vegetables are softened.

- Pour in the vegetable broth and add the white beans. Stir in the dried thyme and basil. Season with salt and black pepper to taste.

2.
- Bring the mixture to a boil, then reduce the heat and let it simmer for about 10 minutes, allowing the flavors to meld together.
- Stir in the chopped spinach and cook for an additional 2-3 minutes, until the spinach is wilted.

3.
- Stir in the lemon juice if using, adjust seasoning as needed.
- Ladle the soup into bowls and serve hot.

Broccoli Cheddar Soup

Prep time
10 mins

Cook Time
25 mins

Servings
2 per.

Calorie
220 kcal

Ingredients:

- **1** tbsp olive oil
- **1** small onion, finely chopped
- **1** clove garlic, minced
- **2** cups broccoli florets
- **1** medium carrot, peeled and grated
- **2** cups low-sodium vegetable broth
- **1** cup low-fat milk (1% or skim)

- **1** tbsp whole wheat flour
- **1** cup shredded low-fat cheddar cheese
- **1/4** tsp black pepper
- **1/4** tsp nutmeg (optional)
- **2** tbsp chopped fresh parsley (optional for garnish)

Instructions:

1.
- Chop the onion and garlic.
- Grate the carrot & cut the broccoli into small florets.

2.
- In a large pot, heat the olive oil over medium heat.
- Add the chopped onion and garlic. Sauté until the onion is translucent, about 3-4 minutes.
- Add the grated carrot and broccoli florets. Cook for another 3-4 minutes.

2.

- Pour in the vegetable broth. Bring to a boil, then reduce the heat and simmer until the broccoli is tender, about 10 minutes.

- Use an immersion blender to puree the soup until smooth. Alternatively, carefully transfer the soup to a blender and blend until smooth, then return it to the pot.

3.

- In a small bowl, whisk together the milk and whole wheat flour until smooth.

- Gradually stir the milk mixture into the soup. Cook over low heat, stirring constantly, until the soup thickens, about 5 minutes.

- Stir in the shredded low-fat cheddar cheese until melted and smooth.

4.

- Season with black pepper and nutmeg if using.

- Ladle the soup into bowls.

- Garnish with chopped fresh parsley if desired.

Red Lentil Soup

Prep time
10 mins

Cook Time
30 mins

Servings
2 per.

Calorie
250 kcal

Ingredients:

- **1** cup red lentils

- **1** medium onion, finely chopped

- **2** carrots, diced

- **2** celery stalks, diced

- **3** garlic cloves, minced

- **1** tbsp olive oil

- **1** tsp ground cumin

- **1** tsp ground coriander

- **1/2** tsp ground turmeric

- **1/2** tsp paprika

- **1/4** tsp cayenne pepper (optional, for a bit of heat)

- **4** cups low-sodium vegetable broth

- **1** cup water

- **1** can (14.5 oz) diced tomatoes, with juice

- **1** bay leaf

- ***** Salt and pepper to taste

- **2** tbsp fresh lemon juice

- **2** tbsp fresh parsley, chopped (for garnish)

Instructions:

1.

- Rinse the red lentils under cold water until the water runs clear. Set aside.

- In a large pot, heat the olive oil over medium heat. Add the chopped onion, carrots, and celery. Sauté until the vegetables are softened, about 5-7 minutes.

- Add the minced garlic, cumin, coriander, turmeric, paprika, and cayenne pepper (if using). Cook for another 1-2 minutes until fragrant.

2.

- Stir in the lentils, vegetable broth, water, diced tomatoes (with their juice), and bay leaf. Bring the mixture to a boil.

- Once boiling, reduce the heat to low and let it simmer uncovered for about 20-25 minutes, or until the lentils and vegetables are tender.

- Remove the bay leaf. Using an immersion blender, blend the soup to your desired consistency. For a chunkier texture, blend just a little; for a smoother soup, blend more thoroughly.

3.

- Stir in the fresh lemon juice and season with salt and pepper to taste.

- Ladle the soup into bowls and garnish with chopped parsley.

Cauliflower Soup

Prep time
10 mins

Cook Time
30 mins

Servings
2 per.

Calorie
150 kcal

Ingredients:

- **1** medium head of cauliflower, chopped

- **1** medium onion, chopped

- **2** cloves garlic, minced

- **2** cups low-sodium vegetable broth

- **1** cup unsweetened almond milk

- **1** tbsp olive oil

- **1** tsp thyme (fresh or dried)

- **1** tsp turmeric

- **1/2** tsp black pepper

- * Salt to taste

- **1** tbsp nutritional yeast (optional, for a cheesy flavor)

- * Fresh parsley for garnish

Instructions:

1.
- Chop the cauliflower into small florets.
- Dice the onion and mince the garlic.
- In a large pot, heat the olive oil over medium heat.
- Add the chopped onion and cook until translucent, about 5 minutes.
- Add the minced garlic and cook for another 1-2 minutes.

2.
- Add the chopped cauliflower to the pot.
- Sprinkle with thyme, turmeric, black pepper, and a pinch of salt.
- Stir to combine and cook for another 2-3 minutes.
- Pour in the low-sodium vegetable broth and almond milk.
- Bring the mixture to a boil, then reduce the heat and let it simmer for 20 minutes, or until the cauliflower is tender.

3.
- Using an immersion blender, blend the soup until smooth and creamy. Alternatively, transfer the soup to a blender in batches and blend until smooth.
- If using nutritional yeast, add it now and blend to incorporate.
- Taste the soup and adjust the seasoning with more salt and pepper if needed.
- Ladle the soup into bowls.
- Garnish with fresh parsley.

Pumpkin Soup

Prep time	Cook Time	Servings	Calorie
15 mins	30 mins	2 per.	150 kcal

Ingredients:

- **1** small pumpkin (about 2 cups cubed)
- **1** medium onion, chopped
- **2** cloves garlic, minced
- **1** tbsp olive oil
- **1** tsp ground cumin
- **1** tsp ground coriander
- **1/2** tsp ground cinnamon
- **1/2** tsp ground turmeric

- **3** cups low-sodium vegetable broth
- **1** cup unsweetened almond milk
- **1** tsp fresh ginger, grated
- * Salt and pepper to taste
- * Fresh parsley for garnish (optional)

Instructions:

1.
- Peel and cube the pumpkin into small pieces.

- In a large pot, heat the olive oil over medium heat. Add the chopped onion and sauté until it becomes translucent, about 5 minutes. Add the minced garlic and sauté for another 1-2 minutes.

- Stir in the ground cumin, coriander, cinnamon, and turmeric. Cook for another minute until the spices become fragrant.

2.
- Add the cubed pumpkin to the pot and stir well to coat with the spices. Cook for about 5 minutes.

- Pour in the low-sodium vegetable broth. Bring the mixture to a boil, then reduce the heat and let it simmer until the pumpkin is tender, about 20 minutes.

- Use an immersion blender to puree the soup until smooth. Alternatively, transfer the soup to a blender in batches and blend until smooth, then return it to the pot.

3.
- Stir in the unsweetened almond milk and grated fresh ginger. Heat through, but do not let it boil.

- Season with salt and pepper to taste. Ladle the soup into bowls, garnish with fresh parsley if desired, and serve hot.

Zucchini Basil Soup

Prep time	Cook Time	Servings	Calorie
10 mins	20 mins	2 per.	120 kcal

Ingredients:

- **2** medium zucchinis, chopped
- **1** medium onion, chopped
- **2** cloves garlic, minced
- **1** cup fresh basil leaves, chopped

- **3** cups low-sodium vegetable broth
- **1** tbsp olive oil
- **1** tsp lemon juice
- ***** Salt and pepper to taste
- **1/2** cup unsweetened almond milk (or any plant-based milk)
- **1/4** tsp red pepper flakes (optional)

Instructions:

1.
- In a large pot, heat the olive oil over medium heat.
- Add the chopped onion and garlic, and sauté until they are soft and fragrant (about 3-4 minutes).
- Add the chopped zucchini to the pot.
- Pour in the vegetable broth and bring the mixture to a boil.
- Reduce the heat and let it simmer until the zucchini is tender (about 10 minutes).

2.
- Remove the pot from heat and let it cool slightly.
- Using an immersion blender (or transferring to a regular blender in batches), blend the soup until smooth.
- Return the blended soup to the pot.
- Stir in the chopped basil, lemon juice, almond milk, salt, and pepper.
- Add red pepper flakes if using, and heat gently until the soup is warmed through.

3.
- Ladle the soup into bowls.
- Garnish with extra basil leaves if desired.

Chickpea Stew

Prep time
10 mins

Cook Time
25 mins

Servings
2 per.

Calorie
250 kcal

Ingredients:

- **1** cup canned chickpeas, drained & rinsed
- **1** small onion, finely chopped
- **1** medium carrot, diced
- **1** celery stalk, diced
- **2** cloves garlic, minced
- **1** cup low-sodium vegetable broth
- **1** cup canned diced tomatoes (no salt)
- **1** tbsp olive oil
- **1** tsp cumin
- **1** tsp smoked paprika

- **1/2** tsp ground turmeric
- **1/2** tsp black pepper
- **1/4** tsp cayenne pepper (optional)
- **1** bay leaf
- **1** tbsp fresh parsley, chopped (for garnish)
- **1**tbsp lemon juice

Instructions:

1.
- Finely chop the onion.
- Dice the carrot and celery.
- Mince the garlic.
- In a large pot, heat the olive oil over medium heat.

2.
- Add the chopped onion, carrot, and celery. Sauté for about 5 minutes until the vegetables are softened.
- Add the minced garlic and cook for another 1-2 minutes until fragrant.
- Stir in the cumin, smoked paprika, ground turmeric, black pepper, and cayenne pepper (if using). Cook for 1 minute to release the flavors.
- Pour in the low-sodium vegetable broth and canned diced tomatoes.

2.
- Add the drained and rinsed chickpeas and the bay leaf.
- Stir to combine.

3.
- Bring the mixture to a boil, then reduce the heat to low.
- Cover and let it simmer for about 20 minutes, allowing the flavors to meld together.
- Remove the bay leaf.
- Stir in the lemon juice.
- Ladle the stew into bowls.
- Garnish with fresh parsley.

Black Bean and Sweet Potato Stew

Prep time
15 mins

Cook Time
30 mins

Servings
2 per.

Calorie
350 kcal

Ingredients:

- **1** medium sweet potato, peeled and diced
- **1** cup black beans, canned (drained & rinsed)
- **1** small onion, diced
- **1** small bell pepper, diced
- **2** cloves garlic, minced
- **1** cup low-sodium vegetable broth
- **1** can (14.5 oz) diced tomatoes with no salt
- **1** tsp olive oil

- **1** tsp ground cumin
- **1** tsp smoked paprika
- **1/2** tsp chili powder
- **1/4** tsp black pepper
- **1/2** tsp salt (optional)
- **1/4** tsp cayenne pepper (optional)
- **1** tbsp fresh cilantro, chopped
- **1** lime, cut into wedges (for garnish)

Instructions:

1.
- Peel and dice the sweet potato then dice the onion and bell pepper.
- Mince the garlic.
- Drain and rinse the black beans.

2.
- In a large pot, heat the olive oil over medium heat.
- Add the diced onion and bell pepper, and sauté for about 5 minutes until softened.
- Add the minced garlic, cumin, smoked paprika, and chili powder. Cook for another 1-2 minutes until fragrant.

3.
- Add the diced sweet potato to the pot, and stir to coat with the spices.
- Pour in the vegetable broth and diced tomatoes. Stir well to combine.
- Bring the mixture to a boil, then reduce the heat to low.
- Cover and simmer for about 20 minutes, or until the sweet potato is tender.

4.
- Stir in the black beans and continue to cook for another 5 minutes, until the beans are heated through.
- Taste the stew and adjust seasoning with salt, black pepper.
- Ladle the stew into bowls & garnish with fresh cilantro & a lime wedge on the side.

Lentil and Spinach Stew

Prep time	Cook Time	Servings	Calorie
15 mins	35 mins	2 per.	250 kcal

Ingredients:

- 1 cup lentils, rinsed
- 1 tbsp olive oil
- 1 small onion, finely chopped
- 2 cloves garlic, minced
- 1 tsp ground cumin
- 1 tsp ground coriander
- 1 tsp smoked paprika
- 4 cups low-sodium vegetable broth

- 2 cups fresh spinach, chopped
- 1 medium carrot, diced
- 1 stalk celery, diced
- 1 small tomato, chopped
- 1 tbsp lemon juice
- *Salt and pepper to taste
- 1 tbsp fresh parsley, chopped (optional)

Instructions:

1.

- In a large pot, heat 1 Tbsp of olive oil over medium heat.

- Add the chopped onion, diced carrot, and diced celery. Sauté for about 5 minutes until the vegetables begin to soften.

- Stir in the minced garlic, 1 tsp ground cumin, 1 tsp ground coriander, and 1 tsp smoked paprika. Cook for an additional 2 minutes until the spices are fragrant.

2.

- Add the rinsed lentils and 4 cups of low-sodium vegetable broth to the pot. Bring the mixture to a boil, then reduce the heat to low and let it simmer for about 25 minutes until the lentils are tender.

- Stir in the chopped spinach and chopped tomato. Cook for an additional 5 minutes until the spinach is wilted and the tomato is soft.

3.

- Add 1 Tbsp of lemon juice, and season with salt and pepper to taste. If desired, sprinkle with chopped fresh parsley before serving.

Mushroom and Barley Stew

Prep time 15 mins	Cook Time 45 mins	Servings 2 per.	Calorie 250 kcal

Ingredients:

- **1** tbsp olive oil
- **1** medium onion, chopped
- **2** cloves garlic, minced
- **2** cups mushrooms, sliced (button or cremini)
- **1** carrot, diced
- **1** celery stalk, diced
- **1/2** cup pearl barley

- **4** cups low-sodium vegetable broth
- **1** can (14.5 oz) diced tomatoes, undrained
- **1** tsp dried thyme
- **1** tsp dried oregano
- **1** bay leaf
- * Salt and pepper to taste
- **2** tbsp fresh parsley, chopped (optional)

Instructions:

1.
- Heat the olive oil in a large pot over medium heat.
- Add the chopped onion and garlic, and sauté until softened, about 3-4 minutes.
- Add the sliced mushrooms, carrot, and celery. Cook for another 5-7 minutes until the vegetables begin to soften.

2.
- Stir in the pearl barley, ensuring it's well mixed with the vegetables.
- Add the vegetable broth, diced tomatoes (with their juice), thyme, oregano, and bay leaf.
- Bring the mixture to a boil, then reduce the heat to low and let it simmer, covered, for about 45 minutes, or until the barley is tender.

3.
- Season with salt and pepper to taste.
- Remove the bay leaf before serving.
- Garnish with fresh parsley if desired.

Eggplant and Tomato Stew

Prep time
10 mins

Cook Time
30 mins

Servings
2 per.

Calorie
150 kcal

Ingredients:

- **1** medium eggplant, diced
- **2** medium tomatoes, diced
- **1** small onion, finely chopped
- **2** cloves garlic, minced
- **1** bell pepper, diced
- **1** cup low-sodium vegetable broth
- **1** tbsp olive oil
- **1** tsp dried oregano
- **1** tsp dried basil

- **1/2** tsp ground black pepper
- **1/4** tsp salt (optional)
- ***** Fresh basil leaves, for garnish

Instructions:

1.
- Dice the eggplant, tomatoes, and bell pepper.
- Finely chop the onion and mince the garlic.

Cooking:

2.
- Heat the olive oil in a large pot over medium heat.
- Add the chopped onion and minced garlic. Sauté for 3-4 minutes until the onion becomes translucent.
- Add the diced eggplant and bell pepper. Cook for about 5 minutes, stirring occasionally.
- Stir in the diced tomatoes, dried oregano, dried basil, ground black pepper, and salt.
- Pour in the vegetable broth and bring the mixture to a simmer.
- Reduce the heat to low, cover the pot, and let it simmer for about 20 minutes, or until the eggplant is tender.
- Taste and adjust the seasoning if necessary.
- Serve the stew hot, garnished with fresh basil leaves.

Tuscan Bean Stew

Prep time 10 mins	Cook Time 30 mins	Servings 2 per.	Calorie 220 kcal

Ingredients:

- **1** tbsp olive oil
- **1** small onion, finely chopped
- **2** cloves garlic, minced
- **1** medium carrot, diced
- **1** celery stalk, diced
- **1** (14.5 oz) can diced tomatoes, no salt

- **1** (15 oz) can cannellini beans, drained and rinsed
- **2** cups low-sodium vegetable broth
- **1** tsp dried rosemary
- **1** tsp dried thyme
- **1** bay leaf

- **1/2** tsp ground black pepper
- **1** cup chopped kale, stems removed
- **1** tbsp fresh lemon juice
- * Salt to taste (optional)
- * Fresh parsley for garnish (optional)

Instructions:

1.
- Heat the olive oil in a large pot over medium heat.
- Add the chopped onion, garlic, carrot, and celery.
- Cook until the vegetables are tender, about 5-7 minutes.
- Stir in the diced tomatoes and cannellini beans.
- Cook for another 2 minutes to combine the flavors.

2.
- Add the vegetable broth, dried rosemary, dried thyme, bay leaf, and black pepper.
- Bring the mixture to a boil, then reduce the heat and let it simmer for 20 minutes.
- Stir in the chopped kale and cook until wilted, about 5 minutes.
- Add the fresh lemon juice and adjust the seasoning with salt, if needed.
- Remove the bay leaf before serving.
- Garnish with fresh parsley if desired.

Thai Vegetable Stew

Prep time
15 mins

Cook Time
30 mins

Servings
2 per.

Calorie
250 kcal

Ingredients:

- **1** tbsp olive oil
- **1** small onion, finely chopped
- **2** cloves garlic, minced
- **1** tbsp ginger, minced
- **1** small red bell pepper, sliced
- **1** small yellow bell pepper, sliced
- **1** medium carrot, sliced
- **1** small zucchini, sliced
- **1** cup broccoli florets
- **1** cup baby spinach

- **1** cup light coconut milk
- **1** cup low-sodium vegetable broth
- **1** tbsp red curry paste
- **1** tbsp soy sauce (low-sodium)
- **1** tsp turmeric powder
- **1** tsp ground coriander
- **1/2** tsp black pepper
- **1/2** lime, juiced
- ***** Fresh cilantro, for garnish

Instructions:

1.
- In a large pot, heat 1 Tbsp of olive oil over medium heat.
- Add the finely chopped onion, minced garlic, and minced ginger to the pot. Sauté for about 2-3 minutes until fragrant.
- Add the sliced red and yellow bell peppers, sliced carrot, sliced zucchini, and broccoli florets. Cook for another 5-7 minutes until the vegetables begin to soften.

2.
- Pour in 1 cup of light coconut milk and 1 cup of low-sodium vegetable broth. Stir in 1 tbsp of red curry paste, 1 tbsp of low-sodium soy sauce, 1 tsp of turmeric powder, 1 tsp of ground coriander, and 1/2 tsp of black pepper.
- Bring the stew to a simmer. Reduce the heat to low and let it cook for about 20 minutes, allowing the flavors to meld together and the vegetables to become tender.
- Stir in the baby spinach and the juice of half a lime. Cook for an additional 2-3 minutes until the spinach is wilted.
- Ladle the stew into bowls and garnish with fresh cilantro. Serve hot.

Southwestern Stew

Prep time 15 mins	Cook Time 30 mins	Servings 2 per.	Calorie 320 kcal

Ingredients:

- **1** tbsp olive oil
- **1** small onion, diced
- **1** red bell pepper, diced
- **1** green bell pepper, diced
- **2** cloves garlic, minced
- **1** medium sweet potato, peeled & cubed

- **1** can (15 oz) low-sodium black beans, drained and rinsed
- **1** can (15 oz) diced tomatoes, no salt added
- **1** cup low-sodium vegetable broth
- **1** tsp ground cumin
- **1** tsp chili powder
- **1/2** tsp smoked paprika
- **1/4** tsp ground black pepper
- **1/4** tsp salt (optional, to taste)
- **1/2** cup frozen corn kernels
- **1/4** cup chopped fresh cilantro
- * Juice of 1 lime

Instructions:

1.
- In a large pot, heat the olive oil over medium heat.
- Add the diced onion, red bell pepper, and green bell pepper. Sauté for 5-7 minutes until the vegetables are softened.
- Stir in the minced garlic and cook for another 1-2 minutes until fragrant.
- Add the cubed sweet potato to the pot and stir to combine.

2.
- Add the black beans and diced tomatoes to the pot, stirring to mix well.
- Add the vegetable broth, ground cumin, chili powder, smoked paprika, black pepper, and salt (if using). Stir well.
- Bring the mixture to a boil, then reduce the heat to low. Cover the pot and simmer for 20 minutes, or until the sweet potatoes are tender.

3.
- Stir in the frozen corn and cook for an additional 5 minutes.
- Remove the pot from heat. Stir in the chopped cilantro and lime juice.
- Serve the stew warm, garnished with extra cilantro if desired.

Caribbean Vegetable Stew

Prep time 15 mins	⏳ Cook Time 30 mins	🍽 Servings 2 per.	⚡ Calorie 350 kcal

Ingredients:

- **1** tablespoon (tbsp) olive oil
- **1** medium onion, diced

- **2** cloves garlic, minced
- **1** teaspoon (tsp) ground cumin
- **1** tsp ground coriander
- **1/2** tsp turmeric
- **1/2** tsp smoked paprika
- **1** medium sweet potato, peeled and cubed
- **1** medium zucchini, diced
- **1** red bell pepper, diced
- **1** cup chopped tomatoes (canned or fresh)
- **1** cup low-sodium vegetable broth
- **1/2** cup coconut milk (light)
- **1** cup cooked chickpeas (or 1 can, drained and rinsed)
- **1/2** cup frozen peas
- **1/4** cup fresh cilantro, chopped
- * Juice of 1 lime
- * Salt and pepper to taste

Instructions:

1.
- In a large pot, heat the olive oil over medium heat.
- Add the diced onion and cook until softened, about 5 minutes.
- Add the minced garlic and cook for another minute.

2.
- Stir in the ground cumin, coriander, turmeric, and smoked paprika. Cook for 1-2 minutes until fragrant.
- Add the sweet potato, zucchini, red bell pepper, chopped tomatoes, vegetable broth, and coconut milk. Stir to combine.
- Bring the mixture to a boil, then reduce heat to low and simmer for 20 minutes, or until the vegetables are tender.

3.
- Stir in the cooked chickpeas and frozen peas. Cook for an additional 5 minutes until heated through.
- Stir in the fresh cilantro and lime juice. Season with salt and pepper to taste.
- Serve hot and enjoy your heart-healthy Caribbean Vegetable Stew!

07

Salads
& dressings

Mediterranean Quinoa Salad

Prep time
15 mins

Cook Time
15 mins

Servings
2 per.

Calorie
320 kcal

Ingredients for Salad:

- **1/2** cup quinoa
- **1** cup water
- **1/2** cup cherry tomatoes, halved
- **1/2** cup cucumber, diced
- **1/4** cup red onion, finely chopped
- **1/4** cup Kalamata olives, pitted and sliced
- **1/4** cup feta cheese, crumbled
- **1/4** cup parsley, chopped

Ingredients for Dressing:

- **2** tbsp extra-virgin olive oil
- **1** tbsp lemon juice
- **1** tsp red wine vinegar
- **1/2** tsp dried oregano
- ***** Salt and pepper to taste

Instructions:

1.
- Rinse the quinoa under cold water.
- In a medium saucepan, bring 1 cup of water to a boil.
- Add the quinoa, reduce heat to low, cover, and simmer for 15 minutes or until the water is absorbed and the quinoa is tender.
- Fluff the quinoa with a fork and let it cool.

2.
- While the quinoa is cooking, halve the cherry tomatoes, dice the cucumber, finely chop the red onion, slice the Kalamata olives, crumble the feta cheese, & chop the parsley.
- In a large bowl, whisk together the olive oil, lemon juice, red wine vinegar, dried oregano, salt, & pepper. Then combine the cooked quinoa, cherry tomatoes, cucumber, red onion, olives, feta cheese, & parsley.
- Pour the dressing over the salad and toss to coat evenly.
- Serve the salad immediately or refrigerate it for up to an hour to let the flavors meld.

Spinach and Berry Salad

Prep time
10 mins

Cook Time
15 mins

Servings
2 per.

Calorie
250 kcal

Ingredients for Salad:

- **4** cups fresh spinach leaves, washed & dried
- **1** cup mixed berries (strawberries, blueberries, raspberries)
- **1/4** cup sliced almonds, toasted
- **1/4** cup crumbled feta cheese
- **1/4** red onion, thinly sliced
- **1/4** cup balsamic vinaigrette (store-bought or homemade)

Ingredients for homemade vinaigrette:

- **2** tbsp balsamic vinegar
- **1** tbsp honey
- **1** tsp Dijon mustard
- **3** tbsp extra-virgin olive oil
- ***** Salt and pepper to taste

Prepare the Vinaigrette (if homemade):

- In a small bowl, whisk together balsamic vinegar, honey, and Dijon mustard.
- Slowly drizzle in the olive oil while whisking continuously until the mixture is well combined.
- Season with salt and pepper to taste. Set aside.

Prepare the Salad:

- Place the spinach leaves in a large salad bowl.
- Add the mixed berries, sliced almonds, crumbled feta cheese, and red onion on top of the spinach.
- Drizzle the balsamic vinaigrette over the salad.
- Toss gently to combine, ensuring the spinach leaves are well coated with the dressing. Then divide the salad into two portions & serve.

Kale and Sweet Potato Salad

Prep time
15 mins

Cook Time
25 mins

Servings
2 per.

Calorie
350 kcal

Ingredients:

- **2** cups kale, chopped
- **1** medium sweet potato, peeled & cubed
- **1/2** cup cherry tomatoes, halved
- **1/4** cup red onion, thinly sliced
- **1/4** cup feta cheese, crumbled
- **1/4** cup walnuts, toasted

- **1** tbsp olive oil
- **1** tbsp balsamic vinegar
- **1** tsp honey
- **1/2** tsp Dijon mustard
- ***** Salt and pepper to taste

Instructions:

1.
- Preheat your oven to 400°F (200°C).
- Toss the cubed sweet potatoes with a bit of olive oil, salt, and pepper.
- Spread them on a baking sheet in a single layer.
- Roast for 20-25 minutes, or until tender and slightly crispy on the edges. Let them cool.

2.
- While the sweet potatoes are roasting, prepare the kale.
- Remove the tough stems and chop the leaves into bite-sized pieces.
- Massage the kale with a small amount of olive oil to soften it.
- In a large bowl, combine the massaged kale, cherry tomatoes, red onion, roasted sweet potatoes, feta cheese, and toasted walnuts.

3.
- In a small bowl, whisk together 1 tbsp of olive oil, 1 tbsp of balsamic vinegar, 1 tsp of honey, 1/2 tsp of Dijon mustard, salt, and pepper.
- Pour the dressing over the salad and toss well to combine.
- Divide the salad into two bowls or plates & serve.

Avocado and Citrus Salad

Prep time
15 mins

Cook Time
0 mins

Servings
2 per.

Calorie
320 kcal

Ingredients:

- **1** large ripe avocado, diced
- **1** grapefruit, segmented
- **1** orange, segmented
- **2** cups mixed greens (such as spinach, arugula, and kale)
- **1/4** cup red onion, thinly sliced
- **1/4** cup feta cheese, crumbled

- **2** tbsp extra-virgin olive oil
- **1** tbsp freshly squeezed lemon juice
- **1** tbsp freshly squeezed orange juice
- **1** tsp honey
- ***** Salt and pepper to taste
- **1** tbsp chopped fresh mint (optional)
- **1** tbsp chopped fresh cilantro (optional)

Instructions:

1.
- In a small bowl, whisk together the extra-virgin olive oil, lemon juice, orange juice, honey, salt, and pepper until well combined.
- In a large salad bowl, combine the mixed greens, avocado, grapefruit segments, orange segments, and red onion.

2.
- Pour the dressing over the salad and gently toss to coat all ingredients evenly.
- Sprinkle the feta cheese, fresh mint, and cilantro (if using) over the top of the salad.
- Divide the salad into two bowls and serve immediately.

Lentil and Beet Salad

Prep time
15 mins

Cook Time
40 mins

Servings
2 per.

Calorie
300 kcal

Ingredients for Salad:

- **1/2** cup dried green or brown lentils
- **2** medium beets, roasted and diced
- **1** small red onion, thinly sliced
- **1/2** cup crumbled feta cheese (optional)
- **1/4** cup chopped fresh parsley
- **1/4** cup chopped walnuts, toasted

Dressing:

- **3** tbsp olive oil
- **2** tbsp balsamic vinegar
- **1** tsp Dijon mustard
- **1** tsp honey (optional)
- ***** Salt and pepper to taste

Instructions:

1.
- Rinse 1/2 cup of dried lentils under cold water.
- In a medium saucepan, combine the lentils with 1 1/2 cups of water.
- Bring to a boil, then reduce the heat and simmer for 20-25 minutes or until the lentils are tender but not mushy.
- Drain and set aside to cool.

2.
- Preheat your oven to 400°F (200°C).
- Wash and scrub the beets, then wrap them in aluminum foil.
- Place the wrapped beets on a baking sheet and roast for 30-35 minutes or until they are fork-tender.
- Allow the beets to cool, then peel and dice them into bite-sized pieces.

3.
- In a small bowl, whisk together 3 tbsp of olive oil, 2 tbsp of balsamic vinegar, 1 tsp of Dijon mustard, and 1 tsp of honey (if using).
- Season with salt and pepper to taste.

4.
- In a large mixing bowl, combine the cooked lentils, diced beets, thinly sliced red onion, and chopped parsley.
- Pour the dressing over the salad and toss gently to combine.
- Top with crumbled feta cheese and toasted walnuts.
- Divide the salad evenly between two plates & serve.

Edamame and Farro Salad

Prep time
10 mins

Cook Time
30 mins

Servings
2 per.

Calorie
350 kcal

Ingredients:

- **1/2** cup farro
- **1** cup shelled edamame (fresh or frozen)
- **1/2** cup cherry tomatoes, halved
- **1/4** cup diced red onion
- **1/4** cup chopped fresh parsley
- **1/4** cup crumbled feta cheese (optional

for lower sodium)

- **2** tbsp extra-virgin olive oil
- **1** tbsp lemon juice
- **1** tsp Dijon mustard
- **1** clove garlic, minced
- * Salt and pepper to taste

Instructions:

1.
- Rinse the farro under cold water. In a medium saucepan, combine the farro with 1 1/2 cups of water. Bring to a boil, then reduce heat to low and simmer for about 25-30 minutes, or until the farro is tender. Drain any excess water and let it cool.

- If using frozen edamame, cook according to package instructions. If fresh, bring a pot of water to a boil, add the edamame, and cook for 5 minutes. Drain and let cool.

2.
- In a large bowl, combine the cooled farro, edamame, cherry tomatoes, red onion, and parsley.

- In a small bowl, whisk together the olive oil, lemon juice, Dijon mustard, and minced garlic. Season with salt and pepper to taste.

3.
- Pour the dressing over the salad and toss to combine. Sprinkle with feta cheese if desired.

- Refrigerate the salad for at least 15 minutes before serving to allow the flavors to meld.

Chickpea and Cucumber Salad

Prep time
15 mins

Cook Time
0 mins

Servings
2 per.

Calorie
200 kcal

Ingredients:

- **1** cup canned chickpeas, rinsed & drained
- **1** large cucumber, diced
- **1** small red onion, finely chopped
- **1/2** cup cherry tomatoes, halved
- **1/4** cup fresh parsley, chopped
- **2** tbsp olive oil
- **1** tbsp lemon juice
- **1** tsp ground cumin
- **1/2** tsp salt
- **1/4** tsp black pepper
- **1/4** cup feta cheese, crumbled (optional)

Instructions:

1.
- Dice the cucumber, finely chop the red onion, and halve the cherry tomatoes.
- In a large bowl, mix the chickpeas, cucumber, red onion, cherry tomatoes, & fresh parsley.
- In a small bowl, whisk together the olive oil, lemon juice, ground cumin, salt, and black pepper.

2.
- Pour the dressing over the chickpea mixture and toss gently to combine.
- If desired, sprinkle crumbled feta cheese on top.
- Serve immediately or refrigerate for an hour to let the flavors meld together.

Broccoli and Apple Salad

Prep time
15 mins

Cook Time
0 mins

Servings
2 per.

Calorie
200 kcal

Ingredients for Salad:

- **1** cup broccoli florets, chopped
- **1** apple, diced
- **1/4** cup red onion, finely chopped
- **1/4** cup dried cranberries
- **1/4** cup walnuts, chopped
- **2** tbsp Greek yogurt
- **1** tbsp apple cider vinegar
- **1** tbsp honey
- **1** tsp Dijon mustard
- ***** Salt and pepper to taste

Instructions:

1.
- Wash and chop the broccoli into small florets.
- Dice the apple into small pieces, leaving the skin on for extra fiber.
- Finely chop the red onion.
- Roughly chop the walnuts.

2.
- In a small bowl, combine the Greek yogurt, apple cider vinegar, honey, and Dijon mustard.
- Mix well until smooth.
- Season with salt and pepper to taste.

3.
- In a large mixing bowl, combine the broccoli, apple, red onion, dried cranberries, and walnuts.
- Pour the dressing over the salad and toss until everything is well coated.
- Let the salad chill in the refrigerator for at least 30 minutes to allow the flavors to meld together.
- Serve cold and enjoy!

Roasted Vegetable and Quinoa Salad

Prep time	Cook Time	Servings	Calorie
15 mins	25 mins	2 per.	350 kcal

Ingredients for Salad:

- **1** cup quinoa
- **2** cups water
- **1** red bell pepper, chopped
- **1** yellow bell pepper, chopped
- **1** zucchini, chopped
- **1** red onion, chopped
- **1** cup cherry tomatoes, halved
- **2** tbsp olive oil
- **1** tsp garlic powder
- **1** tsp dried oregano
- **1** tsp dried basil
- ***** Salt and pepper to taste
- **1/4** cup fresh parsley, chopped

For the Dressing:

- **2** tbsp olive oil
- **1** tbsp balsamic vinegar
- **1** tsp Dijon mustard
- **1** tsp honey
- ***** Salt and pepper to taste

Instructions:

1.
- Rinse the quinoa under cold water.
- In a medium pot, bring 2 cups of water to a boil.
- Add the quinoa, reduce the heat to low, cover, and simmer for about 15 minutes or until the water is absorbed and the quinoa is tender.
- Fluff the quinoa with a fork and set aside to cool.

2.
- Preheat the oven to 400°F (200°C).
- In a large bowl, combine the chopped red bell pepper, yellow bell pepper, zucchini, red onion, and cherry tomatoes.
- Drizzle with 2 tbsp of olive oil and sprinkle with garlic powder, dried oregano, dried basil, salt, and pepper.
- Toss to coat the vegetables evenly.
- Spread the vegetables on a baking sheet in a single layer.
- Roast in the preheated oven for 20-25 minutes, stirring halfway through, until the vegetables are tender and slightly caramelized.

3.
- In a small bowl, whisk together 2 tbsp of olive oil, balsamic vinegar, Dijon mustard, honey, salt, and pepper until well combined.

3.
- In a large bowl, combine the cooked quinoa and roasted vegetables.
- Drizzle the dressing over the salad and toss gently to combine.
- Garnish with chopped fresh parsley & serve.

Avocado Lime Dressing

Prep time
10 mins

Cook Time
0 mins

Servings
2 per.

Calorie
150 kcal

Ingredients:

- **1** ripe avocado
- **2** tbsp fresh lime juice (about 1-2 limes)
- **2** tbsp olive oil
- **1** tbsp Greek yogurt (optional for creaminess)
- **1** garlic clove, minced
- 1/4 tsp salt

- 1/4 tsp black pepper
- 1/4 cup fresh cilantro leaves (optional)
- **2-3** tbsp water (adjust for desired consistency)

Instructions:

1.
- Cut the avocado in half, remove the pit, and scoop out the flesh.
- In a blender or food processor, combine the avocado, lime juice, olive oil, Greek yogurt (if using), minced garlic, salt, and pepper. Blend until smooth.
- Add water, one tablespoon at a time, until the dressing reaches your desired consistency.

2.
- If using cilantro, add it to the blender and pulse until finely chopped and well incorporated.
- Taste the dressing and adjust the seasoning if necessary.
- Pour the dressing into a serving container. Use immediately or store in an airtight container in the refrigerator for up to 2 days.

Cilantro Lime Vinaigrette

Prep time
10 mins

Cook Time
0 mins

Servings
2 per.

Calorie
90 kcal

Ingredients:

- **1** cup fresh cilantro leaves (packed)
- **1/4** cup extra virgin olive oil
- **2** tbsp fresh lime juice (about 1 lime)
- **1** tbsp apple cider vinegar
- **1** tsp honey or agave syrup

- **1** clove garlic, minced
- **1/4** tsp salt
- **1/4** tsp black pepper
- **1/4** tsp ground cumin (optional)
- **2** tbsp water (adjust for consistency)

Instructions:

1.
- Wash and dry the cilantro leaves thoroughly. Remove any large stems.
- In a blender or food processor, combine the cilantro, olive oil, lime juice, apple cider vinegar, honey, garlic, salt, pepper, and cumin (if using).
- Blend until smooth. If the mixture is too thick, add water 1 tbsp at a time until the desired consistency is reached.

2.
- Taste the vinaigrette and adjust seasoning if necessary. Add more lime juice or salt to taste.
- Transfer the vinaigrette to a glass jar or container with a lid. Store in the refrigerator for up to a week. Shake well before using.

Lemon Herb Vinaigrette

Prep time
10 mins

Cook Time
0 mins

Servings
2 per.

Calorie
100 kcal

Ingredients:

- **4** tbsp extra-virgin olive oil
- **2** tbsp fresh lemon juice (about 1 lemon)
- **1** tsp Dijon mustard
- **1** tsp honey (optional for a touch of sweetness)
- **1** small garlic clove, minced
- **1** tbsp fresh parsley, finely chopped
- **1** tbsp fresh basil, finely chopped
- **1** tbsp fresh chives, finely chopped
- ***** Salt and freshly ground black pepper

Instructions:

1.
- In a small mixing bowl, whisk together the lemon juice, Dijon mustard, honey (if using), and minced garlic until well combined.
- Slowly drizzle in the olive oil while continuing to whisk, ensuring the mixture emulsifies and thickens slightly.

2.
- Stir in the chopped parsley, basil, and chives.
- Season with salt and freshly ground black pepper to taste.
- Transfer the vinaigrette to a small jar or container with a tight-fitting lid. Shake well before each use.

Apple Cider Vinaigrette

Prep time
10 mins

Cook Time
0 mins

Servings
2 per.

Calorie
80 kcal

Ingredients:

- **1/4** cup apple cider vinegar
- **1/4** cup extra virgin olive oil
- **1** tbsp Dijon mustard
- **1** tbsp honey
- **1** garlic clove, minced
- **1/2** tsp salt
- **1/4** tsp black pepper

Instructions:

1.

- In a small mixing bowl, combine the apple cider vinegar, Dijon mustard, honey, minced garlic, salt, and black pepper.

- Slowly whisk in the extra virgin olive oil until the vinaigrette is well combined and emulsified.

2.

- Taste and adjust the seasoning if necessary.

- Transfer the vinaigrette to a jar with a tight-fitting lid and refrigerate for at least 30 minutes before serving to allow the flavors to meld.

Greek Yogurt Ranch

 Prep time
10 mins

 Cook Time
0 mins

 Servings
2 per.

 Calorie
60 kcal

Ingredients:

- **1** cup Greek yogurt (non-fat)
- **2** tbsp fresh lemon juice
- **1** tbsp olive oil
- **1** clove garlic, minced
- **1** tbsp fresh dill, chopped (or 1 tsp dried dill)
- **1** tbsp fresh chives, chopped
- **1** tbsp fresh parsley, chopped

- **1** tsp onion powder
- **1/2** tsp garlic powder
- **1/2** tsp salt
- **1/4** tsp black pepper
- **1–2** tbsp water (optional, for desired consistency)

Instructions:

1.

- In a medium bowl, add the Greek yogurt, lemon juice, olive oil, and minced garlic. Stir to combine.

- Mix in the dill, chives, parsley, onion powder, garlic powder, salt, and black pepper.

2.

- If the dressing is too thick, add water, one tablespoon at a time, until the desired consistency is reached.

2.
- Chill the dressing in the refrigerator for at least 30 minutes before serving to allow the flavors to meld.

Chimichurri Sauce

 Prep time
15 mins

 Cook Time
0 mins

 Servings
2 per.

 Calorie
120 kcal

Ingredients:

- **1/2** cup fresh parsley, finely chopped
- **1/4** cup fresh cilantro, finely chopped
- **3** cloves garlic, minced
- **1/4** cup red wine vinegar
- **1/2** cup extra virgin olive oil

- **1** tsp red pepper flakes (optional)
- **1** tsp dried oregano
- **1/2** tsp salt
- **1/4** tsp black pepper
- ***** Juice of 1 lemon

Instructions:

- Finely chop the parsley and cilantro.
- Mince the garlic.
- In a medium bowl, combine parsley, cilantro, and garlic.
- Add red wine vinegar, extra virgin olive oil, and lemon juice to the bowl.

- Add red pepper flakes, oregano, salt, and black pepper.
- Mix all ingredients thoroughly until well combined.
- Let the chimichurri sit for at least 15 minutes to allow flavors to meld.

Miso Ginger Dressing

Prep time
10 mins

Cook Time
0 mins

Servings
2 per.

Calorie
60 kcal

Ingredients:

- **2** tbsp white miso paste
- **2** tbsp rice vinegar
- **1** tbsp soy sauce (low sodium)
- **1** tbsp sesame oil
- **1** tbsp honey

- **1** tbsp fresh ginger, finely grated
- **1** clove garlic, minced
- **2** tbsp water
- **1** tsp sesame seeds (optional)

Instructions:

1.
- Finely grate the fresh ginger.
- Mince the garlic.
- In a small bowl, whisk together the white miso paste, rice vinegar, soy sauce, sesame oil, and honey until smooth.

2.
- Add the grated ginger and minced garlic to the mixture. Whisk again until everything is well combined.
- Gradually add water to the dressing, 1 tbsp at a time, whisking until you reach your desired consistency.
- Sprinkle sesame seeds over the dressing for an added touch of flavor and texture.

Turmeric Tahini Dressing

Prep time
10 mins

Cook Time
0 mins

Servings
2 per.

Calorie
110 kcal

Ingredients:

- **1/4** cup tahini
- **1/4** cup water
- **2** tbsp fresh lemon juice (about half a lemon)
- **1** tbsp extra virgin olive oil
- **1** tbsp apple cider vinegar
- **1** tbsp maple syrup or honey

- **1** tsp ground turmeric
- **1/2** tsp ground cumin
- **1/4** tsp ground black pepper
- **1/4** tsp sea salt (optional)
- **1** small clove garlic, minced

Instructions:

1.
- Measure and gather all ingredients. Mince the garlic if not already done.
- In a medium bowl, whisk together the tahini and water until smooth.
- Add the fresh lemon juice and extra virgin olive oil. Whisk until well combined.

2.
- Add the apple cider vinegar and maple syrup (or honey). Whisk thoroughly.
- Add the ground turmeric, ground cumin, ground black pepper, and sea salt (if using). Whisk until all ingredients are well blended.
- Finally, add the minced garlic and mix well.

3.
- If the dressing is too thick, add more water, 1 tsp at a time, until the desired consistency is reached.
- Serve immediately or store in an airtight container in the refrigerator for up to one week. Shake or stir before using if the dressing separates.

Hummus/with mushrooms

Prep time	Cook Time	Servings	Calorie
10 mins	0-10 mins	2 per.	200-250 kcal

Ingredients:

- **1** can (15 oz) chickpeas (drained and rinsed)
- **2** cloves garlic

- **2** tbsp tahini
- **1** tbsp extra-virgin olive oil

- **1** tbsp lemon juice
- **1/2** tsp ground cumin
- **1/4** tsp salt (or to taste)
- **2–3** tbsp water (for desired consistency)

For the Mushrooms Variant:

- **1** cup mushrooms (sliced)
- **1/2** tbsp extra-virgin olive oil
- **1** clove garlic (minced)
- **1/4** tsp thyme (dried or fresh)
- **1/4** tsp salt (or to taste)
- **1/8** tsp black pepper (or to taste)

Instructions for the Hummus:

- Add the chickpeas, garlic, tahini, olive oil, lemon juice, cumin, and salt to a food processor.
- Blend until smooth. Add water gradually until you achieve the desired consistency.
- Transfer to a serving bowl and garnish with a drizzle of olive oil and a sprinkle of paprika if desired.

Instructions for the Mushrooms:

- Heat olive oil in a skillet over medium heat.
- Add garlic and sauté until fragrant (about 1 minute).
- Add sliced mushrooms, thyme, salt, and pepper. Cook until mushrooms are tender and browned (about 5-7 minutes).
- Fold the sautéed mushrooms into the prepared hummus base.
- Transfer to a serving bowl and garnish with a few mushroom slices and a drizzle of olive oil.

08

Chapter

Desserts

Chia Seed Pudding

Prep time
5 mins

Cook Time
2 hours

Servings
2 per.

Calorie
150 kcal

Ingredients:

- **4** tbsp chia seeds
- **1** cup unsweetened almond milk (or any preferred plant-based milk)
- **1** tsp vanilla extract
- **1-2** tbsp maple syrup or honey (optional)
- *Fresh fruits (e.g., berries, mango, or banana) for topping
- *Nuts and seeds (optional) for topping

Instructions:

1.
- In a medium-sized bowl, combine 4 Tbsp chia seeds and 1 cup unsweetened almond milk.
- Add 1 tsp vanilla extract and 1-2 Tbsp maple syrup or honey if you prefer a sweeter pudding.
- Stir the mixture thoroughly to ensure the chia seeds are evenly distributed and not clumping together.

2.
- Cover the bowl and place it in the refrigerator. Let it sit for at least 2 hours, but for best results, leave it overnight. This allows the chia seeds to absorb the liquid and form a pudding-like consistency.
- After the pudding has set, give it another good stir to break up any clumps & ensure a smooth texture.
- Divide the pudding into two servings. Top with fresh fruits and nuts/seeds of your choice for added flavor and nutrition.

Mango Coconut Chia Pudding

Prep time
5 mins

Cook Time
4 hours

Servings
2 per.

Calorie
150 kcal

Ingredients:

- **1** cup coconut milk (unsweetened)
- **1/2** cup fresh mango puree
- **3** tbsp chia seeds
- **1** tsp vanilla extract
- **1** tbsp honey or maple syrup (optional)
- * Fresh mango slices for garnish
- * Mint leaves for garnish

Instructions:

1.
- In a medium bowl, whisk together the coconut milk, mango puree, chia seeds, vanilla extract, and honey or maple syrup (if using).
- Ensure that the chia seeds are evenly distributed in the liquid to prevent clumping.
- Cover the bowl and place it in the refrigerator. Let it chill for at least 4 hours, or overnight, until it reaches a pudding-like consistency.

2.
- Once the pudding has set, give it a good stir. Divide it into two serving bowls.
- Top with fresh mango slices and a few mint leaves for a refreshing touch.

Coconut Milk Rice Pudding

Prep time
10 mins

Cook Time
40 min

Servings
2 per.

Calorie
250 kcal

Ingredients:

- **1/2** cup brown rice
- **1 1/2** cups water

- **1** cup light coconut milk
- **1/2** cup unsweetened almond milk
- **2** tbsp pure maple syrup
- **1** tsp vanilla extract
- **1/4** tsp ground cinnamon

- **1/4** tsp ground nutmeg
- * Pinch of salt
- * Fresh fruit or nuts for garnish (optional)

Instructions:

1.
- Rinse the brown rice under cold water.
- In a medium saucepan, combine the rice and water. Bring to a boil over medium-high heat.
- Once boiling, reduce the heat to low, cover, and simmer for 20 minutes or until the water is absorbed and the rice is tender.

2.
- In a separate saucepan, combine the light coconut milk, unsweetened almond milk, and pure maple syrup.
- Heat over medium heat, stirring occasionally, until the mixture is warm and well combined.
- Add the cooked rice to the milk mixture.

3.
- Stir in the vanilla extract, ground cinnamon, ground nutmeg, and a pinch of salt.
- Cook over medium-low heat, stirring frequently, for about 20 minutes or until the mixture thickens to a pudding-like consistency.
- Divide the pudding into two bowls.
- Garnish with fresh fruit or nuts if desired.

Oatmeal Banana Cookies

Prep time
10 mins

Cook Time
15-20 min

Servings
2 per.

Calorie
150 kcal

Ingredients:

- **2** ripe bananas

- **1** cup rolled oats

- **1/4** cup almond butter
- **1/4** cup honey
- **1/2** tsp vanilla extract
- **1/2** tsp cinnamon
- **1/4** cup chopped walnuts (optional)
- **1/4** cup raisins (optional)
- ***** Pinch of salt

Instructions:

1.
- Preheat your oven to 350°F (175°C) and line a baking sheet with parchment paper.
- In a medium bowl, mash the ripe bananas until smooth.
- Add the rolled oats, almond butter, honey, vanilla extract, cinnamon, and salt to the mashed bananas. Mix until well combined.

2.
- If using, fold in the chopped walnuts and raisins.
- Scoop tablespoon-sized portions of the mixture onto the prepared baking sheet, flattening them slightly with the back of the spoon.

3.
- Bake in the preheated oven for 15-20 minutes, or until the cookies are golden brown and firm to the touch.
- Allow the cookies to cool on the baking sheet for a few minutes before transferring them to a wire rack to cool completely.

Fresh Apricot Crisp

 Prep time
15 mins

 Cook Time
25 min

 Servings
2 per.

 Calorie
250 kcal

Ingredients:

- **4** fresh apricots, pitted and sliced
- **1/4** cup rolled oats
- **1/4** cup whole wheat flour
- **2** tbsp almond flour
- **2** tbsp honey or maple syrup
- **1** tbsp chia seeds
- **2** tbsp olive oil or coconut oil
- **1/4** tsp cinnamon
- **1/8** tsp nutmeg
- **1/4** tsp vanilla extract

- *A pinch of salt
- 1 tbsp lemon juice
- 2 tbsp chopped almonds or walnuts

Instructions:

1.
- Preheat your oven to 350°F (175°C).
- In a mixing bowl, toss the sliced apricots with lemon juice and set aside.

2.
- In a separate bowl, mix the rolled oats, whole wheat flour, almond flour, chia seeds, cinnamon, nutmeg, and salt.
- Add the honey (or maple syrup), olive oil (or coconut oil), and vanilla extract. Stir until the mixture is crumbly.

3.
- Place the apricot slices in a baking dish.
- Sprinkle the crisp topping evenly over the apricots.
- Add chopped almonds or walnuts on top for extra crunch.

4.
- Place the baking dish in the preheated oven and bake for 25 minutes or until the topping is golden brown and the apricots are bubbly.
- Let the apricot crisp cool for a few minutes before serving.

Almond Butter Chocolate Chip Cookies

Prep time
10 mins

Cook Time
10-15 min

Servings
2 per.

Calorie
150 kcal/ Cookie

Ingredients:

- 1 cup almond butter
- 1/2 cup coconut sugar
- 1 large egg
- 1 tsp vanilla extract
- 1/2 tsp baking soda
- 1/4 tsp salt
- 1/2 cup dark chocolate chips (70% cocoa or higher)

Instructions:

1.

- Preheat your oven to 350°F (175°C) and line a baking sheet with parchment paper.

- In a medium bowl, combine the almond butter, coconut sugar, egg, and vanilla extract. Mix until smooth and creamy.

- Add the baking soda and salt to the mixture and blend well.

2.

- Fold in the dark chocolate chips, ensuring they are evenly distributed throughout the dough.

- Using a tablespoon (Tbsp), scoop the dough and roll it into balls. Place the balls on the prepared baking sheet, spacing them about 2 inches apart. Gently press each ball down to flatten slightly.

3.

- Bake in the preheated oven for 10-12 minutes, or until the edges are golden brown.

- Allow the cookies to cool on the baking sheet for a few minutes before transferring them to a wire rack to cool completely.

Apple and Blackberry Oat Crumble

Prep time	Cook Time	Servings	Calorie
15 mins	25-30 min	2 per.	250-300 kcal

Ingredients:

- **2** medium apples (peeled, cored, and sliced)
- **1** cup blackberries (fresh or frozen)
- **1/2** cup rolled oats
- **2** tbsp almond flour
- **1** tbsp honey or maple syrup

- **1** tbsp coconut oil (melted)
- **1/2** tsp cinnamon
- **1/4** tsp nutmeg
- **1/2** tsp vanilla extract
- **1** tbsp chopped nuts (optional)

Instructions:

- Preheat your oven to 350°F (175°C).

- In a medium bowl, combine the sliced apples and blackberries.

1.
- Add 1/2 tsp of vanilla extract and toss to coat the fruit evenly.
- Place the fruit mixture into a small baking dish.

2.
- In another bowl, mix the rolled oats, almond flour, cinnamon, and nutmeg.
- Add the melted coconut oil and honey (or maple syrup) to the dry ingredients.
- Stir until the mixture becomes crumbly.
- Optionally, add 1 tbsp of chopped nuts for extra texture and nutrition.

3.
- Evenly spread the crumble topping over the fruit mixture in the baking dish.
- Place the baking dish in the preheated oven.
- Bake for 25-30 minutes or until the topping is golden brown and the fruit is bubbling.
- Allow the crumble to cool slightly before serving.
- Serve warm, optionally with a dollop of low-fat yogurt or a splash of almond milk.

Whole Wheat Banana Bread

Prep time 15 mins	Cook Time 50-60 min	Servings 2 per.	Calorie 180 kcal/slice

Ingredients:

- **1** cup whole wheat flour
- **1** cup all-purpose flour
- **1** tsp baking soda
- **1/4** tsp salt
- **1/2** tsp ground cinnamon
- **1/4** tsp ground nutmeg
- **3** ripe bananas, mashed

- **1/3** cup honey
- **1/4** cup unsweetened applesauce
- **2** large eggs
- **1** tsp vanilla extract
- **1/4** cup plain Greek yogurt
- **1/4** cup chopped walnuts (optional)

Instructions:

1.

- Preheat your oven to 350°F (175°C). Grease a 9x5-inch loaf pan or line it with parchment paper.

- In a medium bowl, whisk together the whole wheat flour, all-purpose flour, baking soda, salt, cinnamon, and nutmeg.

2.

- In a large bowl, combine the mashed bananas, honey, applesauce, eggs, vanilla extract, and Greek yogurt until well blended.

- Gradually add the dry ingredients to the wet ingredients, mixing just until combined. Be careful not to overmix. Fold in the chopped walnuts if using.

3.

- Pour the batter into the prepared loaf pan and smooth the top. Bake in the preheated oven for 50-60 minutes, or until a toothpick inserted into the center comes out clean.

- Allow the banana bread to cool in the pan for about 10 minutes before transferring it to a wire rack to cool completely.

Whole Wheat Blueberry Pancakes

Prep time	Cook Time	Servings	Calorie
10 mins	20 min	2 per.	250 kcal

Ingredients:

- **1** cup whole wheat flour
- **1** tbsp baking powder
- **1/2** tsp baking soda
- **1/4** tsp salt
- **1** cup low-fat buttermilk

- **1** large egg
- **1** tbsp honey
- **1** tsp vanilla extract
- **1** tbsp olive oil
- **1** cup fresh blueberries

Instructions:

1.

- In a large mixing bowl, whisk together the whole wheat flour, baking powder, baking soda, and salt.

1.
- In a separate bowl, whisk together the buttermilk, egg, honey, vanilla extract, and olive oil until well combined.

- Pour the wet ingredients into the dry ingredients and stir until just combined. Be careful not to overmix; the batter should be slightly lumpy.

2.
- Gently fold in the blueberries.

- Preheat a non-stick skillet or griddle over medium heat. Lightly grease with olive oil or cooking spray if needed.

3.
- Pour 1/4 cup of batter onto the skillet for each pancake. Cook until bubbles form on the surface and the edges look set, about 2-3 minutes. Flip and cook for another 2-3 minutes or until golden brown and cooked through.

- Serve warm, optionally topped with additional fresh blueberries or a light drizzle of honey.

Almond Flour Blueberry Muffins

Prep time
10 mins

Cook Time
20-25 min

Servings
2 per.

Calorie
180 kcal

Ingredients:

- **2** cups almond flour
- **2** large eggs
- **1/4** cup unsweetened almond milk
- **1/4** cup honey or maple syrup
- **2** tbsp coconut oil, melted
- **1** tsp vanilla extract

- **1/2** tsp baking soda
- **1/2** tsp apple cider vinegar
- **1** cup fresh or frozen blueberries
- **1/4** tsp salt
- ***** Optional: 1/2 tsp cinnamon

Instructions:

1.
- Preheat your oven to 350°F (175°C). Line a muffin tin with 6 paper liners or grease the tin with a bit of coconut oil.

- In a large bowl, whisk together the almond flour, baking soda, salt, and optional cinnamon.

2.
- In a separate bowl, beat the eggs and then add the unsweetened almond milk, honey or maple syrup, melted coconut oil, and vanilla extract. Mix until well combined.

- Pour the wet ingredients into the dry ingredients and mix until just combined. Do not overmix.

- Gently fold in the blueberries.

3.
- Divide the batter evenly among the 6 muffin cups, filling them almost to the top.

- Bake for 20-25 minutes, or until a toothpick inserted into the center of a muffin comes out clean.

- Allow the muffins to cool in the tin for 10 minutes, then transfer them to a wire rack to cool completely.

Sweet Potato Brownies

Prep time
15 mins

Cook Time
25-30 min

Servings
2 per.

Calorie
160 kcal

Ingredients:

- **2** medium sweet potatoes (about 2 cups mashed)
- **1/2** cup almond flour
- **1/4** cup unsweetened cocoa powder
- **1/4** cup maple syrup

- **2** tbsp coconut oil, melted
- **1** tsp vanilla extract
- **1/2** tsp baking powder
- **1/4** tsp salt
- **1/2** cup dark chocolate chips (optional)

Equipment Needed:

* Baking sheet
* Fork or potato masher
* Mixing bowls

* Measuring cups and spoons
* 8x8 inch baking pan
* Parchment paper

Instructions:

1.

- Preheat the oven to 350°F (175°C).

- Line an 8x8 inch baking pan with parchment paper or lightly grease it with coconut oil.

- Pierce the sweet potatoes with a fork and bake them on a baking sheet for 45 minutes or until soft. Alternatively, you can microwave them on high for 8-10 minutes, turning them halfway through.

2.

- Once the sweet potatoes are cooked, allow them to cool slightly, then peel and mash them in a large mixing bowl.

- Add the almond flour, unsweetened cocoa powder, maple syrup, melted coconut oil, vanilla extract, baking powder, and salt to the mashed sweet potatoes. Mix until well combined.

- Fold in the dark chocolate chips if using.

- Pour the batter into the prepared baking pan, spreading it evenly with a spatula.

- Bake in the preheated oven for 25-30 minutes, or until a toothpick inserted into the center comes out clean.

Carrot Cake Energy Bites

Prep time 15 mins	Cook Time 0 min	Servings 2 per.	Calorie 100 kcal

Ingredients:

- **1** cup finely grated carrots
- **1** cup rolled oats
- **1/2** cup almond flour
- **1/2** cup unsweetened shredded coconut
- **1/2** cup chopped walnuts
- **1/4** cup raisins
- **1/4** cup maple syrup

- **1/4** cup almond butter
- **1** tsp vanilla extract
- **1** tsp ground cinnamon
- **1/2** tsp ground ginger
- **1/4** tsp ground nutmeg
- **1/4** tsp salt

Instructions:

1.

- In a large mixing bowl, combine the grated carrots, rolled oats, almond flour, shredded coconut, and chopped walnuts.

- Add the raisins, maple syrup, almond butter, vanilla extract, ground cinnamon, ground ginger, ground nutmeg, and salt to the bowl.

2.

- Mix all the ingredients thoroughly until well combined. If the mixture is too dry, add a bit more maple syrup or almond butter.

- Using your hands, form the mixture into small balls, about 1 inch in diameter.

3.

- Place the energy bites on a baking sheet lined with parchment paper.

- Refrigerate the bites for at least 1 hour to allow them to firm up.

Almond Flour Lemon Bars

Prep time
15 mins

Cook Time
25 min

Servings
2 per.

Calorie
150 kcal

For the Crust:

- **1** cup almond flour
- **2** tbsp coconut flour
- **2** tbsp honey
- **1/4** cup melted coconut oil
- **1/4** tsp sea salt

For the Lemon Filling:

- **3** large eggs
- **1/2** cup freshly squeezed lemon juice (about 2-3 lemons)
- **1/4** cup honey
- **1** tbsp lemon zest
- **2** tbsp almond flour

Instructions:

1.

- Preheat your oven to 350°F (175°C). Line an 8x8 inch baking dish with parchment paper.

- In a medium bowl, combine the almond flour, coconut flour, honey, melted coconut oil, and sea salt. Mix until well combined and a dough forms.

1.

- Press the dough evenly into the bottom of the prepared baking dish.

- Bake the crust for 10 minutes, or until it starts to turn golden brown. Remove from the oven and let it cool slightly.

2.

- In a large bowl, whisk together the eggs, lemon juice, honey, lemon zest, and almond flour until smooth and well combined.

- Pour the lemon filling over the pre-baked crust, spreading it out evenly.

- Return the baking dish to the oven and bake for an additional 15 minutes, or until the filling is set and slightly firm to the touch.

3.

- Remove from the oven and allow the lemon bars to cool completely in the baking dish.

- Once cooled, transfer the dish to the refrigerator for at least 1 hour before cutting into squares.

- Cut the chilled lemon bars into squares and serve. Store any leftovers in an airtight container in the refrigerator.

Apple Cinnamon Overnight Oats

Prep time
10 mins

Refrigerate
overnight

Servings
2 per.

Calorie
300 kcal

Ingredients:

- **1** cup rolled oats

- **1** cup unsweetened almond milk (or any plant-based milk)

- **1** small apple, diced

- **2** tbsp chia seeds

- **2** tbsp Greek yogurt (optional for creaminess)

- **1** tsp ground cinnamon

- **1** tsp honey or maple syrup (optional for sweetness)

- **1/4** tsp vanilla extract

- **2** tbsp chopped nuts (e.g., walnuts, almonds) for topping

- **1** tbsp raisins or dried cranberries for topping

Instructions:

1.

- In a medium-sized bowl or a large mason jar, combine the rolled oats, almond milk, chia seeds, Greek yogurt (if using), ground cinnamon, honey or maple syrup (if using), and vanilla extract. Stir well to ensure all ingredients are mixed thoroughly.

- Fold in the diced apple.

- Cover the bowl or seal the mason jar and place it in the refrigerator overnight (or for at least 6 hours).

2.

- In the morning, give the mixture a good stir. If the oats are too thick, you can add a splash of almond milk to reach your desired consistency.

- Serve the oats in bowls and top with chopped nuts and raisins or dried cranberries for extra texture and flavor.

No Bake Cheesecake in a Jar

Prep time
15 mins

Chill Time
1 hour

Servings
2 per.

Calorie
200 kcal

For the Crust:

- **4** graham crackers

- **1** tbsp coconut oil (melted)

For the Topping:

- **1/2** cup mixed berries (blueberries, strawberries, raspberries)

- **1** tsp honey or maple syrup (optional)

For the Cheesecake Filling:

- **1/2** cup low-fat Greek yogurt

- **4** oz (ounces) low-fat cream cheese (softened)

- **1** tbsp honey or maple syrup

- **1/2** tsp (teaspoon) vanilla extract

- **1/2** tsp lemon juice

Prepare the Crust:

1.

- Place the graham crackers in a plastic bag and crush them into fine crumbs .

- Mix the crumbs with the melted coconut oil until well combined.

- Divide the mixture evenly between two jars, pressing it down with the back of a spoon to form the crust layer.

Make the Cheesecake Filling:

- In a medium bowl, mix the low-fat Greek yogurt and softened low-fat cream cheese until smooth.

- Add the honey or maple syrup, vanilla extract, and lemon juice. Mix until well combined.

- Spoon the mixture over the crust in the jars, dividing it evenly between the two.

Add the Topping:

- Wash and dry the mixed berries.

- Divide the berries evenly between the two jars, placing them on top of the cheesecake filling.

- Optionally, drizzle a little honey or maple syrup over the berries for added sweetness.

Chill:

- Cover the jars with lids or plastic wrap.

- Chill in the refrigerator for at least 1 hour before serving.

Homemade Fruit Sorbet

Prep time 15 mins	Freezing Time 2-3 hours	Servings 2 per.	Calorie 120 kcal

Ingredients:

- **2** cups fresh mixed berries (strawberries, blueberries, raspberries)
- **1** medium banana, sliced and frozen

- **1** tbsp honey or agave syrup
- **1** tsp lemon juice
- **1/4** cup water (adjust as needed)

Instructions:

1.
- Wash the berries thoroughly.
- Slice the banana and freeze for at least 2 hours or overnight.
- In a blender, combine the mixed berries, frozen banana slices, honey (or agave syrup), lemon juice, and water.
- Blend until smooth. If the mixture is too thick, add more water, one tablespoon at a time, until you reach the desired consistency.

2.
- Pour the blended mixture into a shallow, freezer-safe container.
- Freeze for 2-3 hours, stirring every 30 minutes to prevent ice crystals from forming and to ensure a smooth texture.
- Once the sorbet is firm but scoopable, serve immediately. If it becomes too hard, let it sit at room temperature for a few minutes before serving.

Banana Ice Cream

Prep time 10 mins	Freezing Time 2 hours	Servings 2 per.	Calorie 200 kcal

Ingredients:

- **4** ripe bananas
- **2** tbsp almond butter (optional)
- **1** tsp vanilla extract
- **1/4** cup unsweetened almond milk or any other plant-based milk

Instructions:

- Peel the bananas and slice them into thin rounds. Place the slices in a single layer on a baking sheet lined with parchment paper.
- Freeze the banana slices for at least 2 hours, or until they are completely frozen.
- Transfer the frozen banana slices to a food processor or high-speed blender. Blend until smooth, stopping to scrape down the sides as needed. This process may take a few minutes.

2.

- Once the bananas are smooth and creamy, add the almond butter and vanilla extract. Blend again until everything is well combined. If the mixture is too thick, add a little almond milk to reach your desired consistency.

- Serve the banana ice cream immediately for a soft-serve texture. For a firmer texture, transfer the mixture to an airtight container and freeze for an additional 1-2 hours.

Berry Greek Yogurt Popsicles

Prep time 10 mins	Freezing Time 4-6 hours	Servings 2 per.	Calorie 100 kcal

Ingredients:

- **1** cup mixed berries (blueberries, strawberries, raspberries)
- **1** cup Greek yogurt (preferably non-fat or low-fat)
- **2** tbsp honey or maple syrup
- **1** tsp vanilla extract
- **2** tbsp chia seeds (optional for extra fiber)

Instructions:

1.

- Wash and dry the berries.
- Slice the strawberries into smaller pieces if they are large.
- In a blender, combine the mixed berries, Greek yogurt, honey or maple syrup, and vanilla extract. Blend until smooth.

2.

- If using chia seeds, stir them into the blended mixture after blending.
- Pour the mixture into popsicle molds, leaving a little space at the top for expansion when freezing.

3.

- Insert the popsicle sticks into the molds.
- Freeze for at least 4-6 hours, or until completely solid.
- To release the popsicles, run the molds under warm water for a few seconds.

09

Shoping List &
Nutrition Guide

Organizing a Heart-Healthy Shopping List

The heart is a crucial organ that needs to be kept healthy at all times, and this can be done easily through the practice of taking healthy meals. Low fat diet is not only effective in heart health but also boosts energy levels, improves general health and leads to healthier, happier and longer life. Despite this, choosing the right food can at times be a challenge given the many choices out in the supermarkets in the present time

This heart-healthy shopping list makes grocery shopping easier for you and ensures that you pick foods that are good for your heart. It emphasizes foods that have healthy nutrients for the heart such as fruits, vegetables, whole grains, lean meats, and low levels of unhealthy fats. When integrated into your daily food plan, these foods can be prepared into tasty and healthy dishes for the heart and body.

Regardless of whether your goal is to reduce your cholesterol levels, maintain proper blood pressure or improve your diet, this guide serves a useful purpose. Here are the basics of heart-healthy foods to learn more about how to choose the healthiest foods for your heart.

Fruits:

- Apples
- Oranges
- Berries (strawberries,
- blueberries, raspberries)
- Bananas
- Grapes
- Pears
- Citrus fruits (lemons, limes)
- Avocado

Vegetables:

- Leafy greens :(spinach, kale,
- Swiss chard)
- Broccoli
- Carrots
- Bell peppers
- Tomatoes
- Cucumbers
- Asparagus
- Brussels sprouts
- Sweet potatoes
- Onions
- Garlic

Whole Grains:

- Oats (steel-cut or rolled oats)
- Whole wheat bread
- Whole grain pasta
- Brown rice
- Quinoa
- Barley
- Whole grain cereals (low sugar)
- Farro

Protein Sources:

- **Lean Meats and Poultry:**
- Skinless chicken breast
- Turkey breast
- **Fish and Seafood:**
- Salmon
- Mackerel
- Sardines
- Tuna
- Shrimp
- **Plant-Based Proteins:**
- Beans (black beans, chickpeas, lentils)
- Tofu
- Tempeh
- Edamame
- Nuts and seeds (almonds, walnuts, chia seeds, flaxseeds)

Dairy:

- Non-fat milk
- Non-fat Greek yogurt
- Non-fat cottage cheese
- Mozzarella cheese (low-fat or part-skim)
- Kefir (low-fat)

Fats and Oils:

- Olive oil
- Canola oil
- Avocado oil
- Nut butters (unsweetened almond or peanut butter)

Beverages:

- Green tea
- Herbal tea
- Water
- Sparkling water (unsweetened)

Spices and Condiments

- Herbs (fresh or dried: basil, oregano, rosemary, thyme)
- Spices (turmeric, cumin, paprika, cinnamon)
- Vinegar (balsamic, apple cider)
- Low-sodium soy sauce
- Mustard

Snacks

- Fresh fruit
- Raw vegetables (carrot sticks, celery sticks)
- Hummus
- Air-popped popcorn
- Whole grain crackers

Miscellaneous

- Whole grain bread crumbs
- Low-sodium vegetable broth
- No-salt-added canned tomatoes
- Dark chocolate (70% cocoa or higher, in moderation)

Nutrition Guide:

Daily portions Based on your Heart healthy lifestyle:

Food Group	Food Item	Daily Portion	Notes
Vegetables	Leafy Greens (spinach, kale)	2-3 cups	Rich in vitamins, minerals, and fiber
	Cruciferous (broccoli, cauliflower)	1-2 cups	Contains heart-healthy antioxidants
	Other Vegetables (carrots, bell peppers)	1-2 cups	Variety of nutrients and fiber
Fruits	Berries (strawberries, blueberries)	1 cup	High in antioxidants and fiber
	Citrus (oranges, grapefruits)	1-2 medium fruits	Good source of vitamin C
	Other Fruits (apples, bananas)	1-2 medium fruits	Provides potassium and fiber
Whole Grains	Oats	1 cup cooked	Can help lower cholesterol
	Quinoa, Brown Rice	1 cup cooked	High in fiber and nutrients
	Whole Wheat Bread	2 slices	Opt for 100% whole grain
Protein	Legumes (beans, lentils)	1-2 cups cooked	High in fiber and protein, low in fat
	Fish (salmon, mackerel)	2 servings (3.5 oz each)	Rich in omega-3 fatty acids
	Nuts (almonds, walnuts)	1 ounce (about 1/4 cup)	Contains healthy fats
Dairy	Low-fat or Fat-free Milk	2-3 cups	Provides calcium and vitamin D

	Yogurt	1-2 cups	Probiotic benefits and calcium
Healthy Fats	Olive Oil	2 tablespoons	Use as a dressing or for cooking
	Avocado	1/2 medium	Provides monounsaturated fats
Beverages	Water	8-10 cups	Essential for overall health
	Green Tea	1-2 cups	Contains antioxidants
Extras	Dark Chocolate	1 ounce	Choose 70% cocoa or higher for heart health benefits
	Flaxseeds, Chia Seeds	1-2 tablespoons	High in omega-3 fatty acids and fiber

Conclusion:

Closing for the final pages of this cookbook filled with recipes for a healthy heart and ideas on how to change your lifestyle for the better, let's recall and celebrate all that we've learned and all the yummy dishes we've come across. This book has been a lot more than the delicious heart friendly recipes, it was the guiding light to a healthier and fuller life.

Heart health is not a one-time event or a bathing suit season; it is an ongoing process of creating a healthy lifestyle plan that includes nutrition as well as exercise and stress reduction. Having adopted the healthy eating habits that include the use of fresh vegetables, fruits, whole grains, lean proteins, and healthy fats in your regular meals has gone a long way in enhancing the health of your heart. It is my hope that every recipe in this cookbook has been well planned and tasted to not only help those with heart problems but also enhance one's health, slim down, and have more energy.

This cookbook has inspired you to take healthy modifications into your kitchen and dining area. The emphasis of the benefits of balanced meals, nutrient density, and the pleasure of creating and consuming meals in the company of loved ones further cements an integrative outlook on well-being. All these practices are helpful in getting a longer, healthier, and more satisfying life. While you read through the recipes and other information given below, always keep in mind that managing your heart health is a lifelong process. The overview of the heart-healthy diet shows that it is a future-oriented and tasty strategy that can be adapted to your requirementment. Whether you are preparing merely a breakfast snack, lunch sandwich, or a lavish dinner, it is a chance to feed one's heart as well as the body.

I am grateful that you have joined me in this journey towards improving heart health through the foods we cook and eat. I hope the recipes and tips provided in this book encourage you to make these adjustments toward better heart health daily. Continue on this path of discovery, discovery and continue to relish each moment of it with as much passion as you have brought to this path. Cheers to many more delicious meals and to the health of your heart – all the best in each step!

Dear Reader,

I hope you enjoyed reading my Heart Healthy Cookbook for beginners. Your support means a lot to me, and I would love to hear your thoughts on the book. If you had a positive experience, could you please take a moment to write a review on the book's listing page on Amazon? Your feedback not only helps me improve but also assists other readers in discovering my work.

Thank you for your time and support!

Marianna S.

Discover Your Exelent Free Bonus!

Thank you for choosing "Heart Healthy Cookbook for Beginners"! To support your journey toward a healthier ′ lifestyle we arranged a bonus availeble for free.

Scan the QR code below
to download these valuable resources:

Don't miss out on these invaluable bonuses! Scan the QR code to download your free Heart healthy-Matirials and continue your Heart healthy journey with confidence and ease. Enjoy healthier life!

If you have any problems to acess the Bonus, please write me to: **milanjabooks@gmail.com**